THE TRADITIONAL WAY

The Mystique and Heritage of Archery

THE TRADITIONAL WAY

The Mystique and Heritage of Archery

by
FRED ANDERSON

Hello Jill,
Thanks for your
friendship — I hope you
enjoy my book.

Fred Anderson

'97

First printed in March 1997

10 9 8 7 6 5 4 3 2 1

Manufactured in the United States of America

TOX PRESS
E. 750 Krabbenhoft Rd.
Grapeview, Washington 98546

ACKNOWLEDGMENTS

I want to recognize and thank all the people who have contributed to this book, Ira Blair, from Southern California, provided many photographs and documents of early archers from the Hugh Rich collection. Joe St. Charles shared some pictures from his Seattle museum archives. The fine Iowa artist, Bill Barringer, allowed me to use his portrait of Howard Hill. Many current, champion caliber archers provided photos: Ed Kellow of British Columbia; John Kellow of British Columbia; Tom Cole of Pennsylvania; Steve Gorr of Washington; Bob Wesley of Mississippi, and Ron LaClair of Michigan. Thanks to Gaylynn Potemkin, the real professional in this project, for using her expertise in marshaling this work through. Being somewhat of an undirected fellow, I could never have done this book without the hours of help and encouragement from my wife, Barbara.

I also want to acknowledge that I am nothing of myself, but all that I have I owe to the great God of us all.

Contents

Acknowledgments 7
Introduction 11

Young Bowmen 13

I. EQUIPMENT Pondering About Bows 17
The Bowyer 29
Yew and Me 35
Some Bow Proverbs 41
Straight Arrows 53
The Cutting Edge 63
Stories That Leave You All Aquiver 69
That String Thing 75

II. SHOOTING How to Shoot the Doggone Thing 81
A-Roving 103
The Shoot 107
Alone 113
The Great Lawn Game 119
Arrowshooting 123

The Bowman 129

III. HUNTING Traditional Bowhunting 133
Therapy of the Hills 141
Them There Goats 145
Oh! The Adventure of it All 151

IV. PROFILES FROM THE DUST   The Golden Chain   163

Profiles   165

    Will Compton; "The Chief"
    Art Young; "The Archer Adventurer"
    Saxton Pope; "Ku Wi, The Medicine Man"
    Howard Hill; "Mr. Archery"
    Ken and Walt Wilhelm; "The Brothers"
    Hugh Rich; "The Arrow Maker"
    Ande Vail; "Mr. Trick Shot"
    Roy Hoff; "Mr. Archery Magazine"
    Frank Eicholtz; "The Father Of The
      Laminated Bow"

The Old Bowman   215

V. PHILOSOPHY   Teen Times   219

Cock O' the Walk   229

The Sylvan Toxophilite   233

Matrimony Tales   237

Kindred Spirits   243

Connections   249

Elderly Bowman   259

Epilogue   263

Order Form   265

Your Notes   267

INTRODUCTION

This book was written to further the understanding and appreciation of the contemporary sport of American traditional archery. Bringing the many diverse aspects of the sport into a coherent entity, it is designed to be utilized by archery dealers to introduce novices into the sport as well as for the reading enjoyment of the experienced bowman. It was developed after over 40 years of active participation in the sport by the author.

There is a need for both new and experienced archers alike to have a basic knowledge of the various facets and history of the sport.. This study will allow the reader to gain a more objective understanding of the hows and whys of the sport and thus gain more insight into his own reactions to it.

Traditional archery is more than just a sport, it involves a frame of mind. Attitudes, values, myths, and legends abound. Herein, the philosophy of the sport is explored through a number of the author's personal experiences. This is subjective, but each archer does approach the sport from his own subjective frame of reference. Subjectivity in the sport is not wrong as long as one can objectively accept the diverse nature of its participants.

The subject matter consists of five major areas organized on the basis of the significant concepts and issues of the sport. Section One deals with the equipment used in contemporary traditional archery. This is broken down into discussions on bows, arrows, broadheads, and quivers. The second section concerns the shooting styles and events of contemporary archery. Various aspects of bow and arrow hunting are discussed in Section Three. The fourth section deals with some historical figures of the sport and emphasizes that in order to be considered "traditional," the sport must have its foundations in history. The philosophy of the sport and the author's personal connection to it constitute the fifth and final section. It is not necessary to follow the content in sequence. The reader is encouraged to pick and choose topics at any point for enjoyment and further understanding.

Few books have been published that are totally complete or accurate in their treatment of the sport. This work should be viewed as a collection of writings that can be revised and updated anytime depending on new and improved information. There are note-taking pages in the back of the book to allow the reader to record these new and improved truths as they are revealed.

Although objectivity is one of the author's goals, he freely admits that a good share of the book's philosophy has been developed by means of suppositions, generalizations, values, and humor derived from the sport's many practitioners. Hopefully, you'll discover that this study is not mean-spirited, especially concerning the compound bow. The compounding sport is legitimate, entertaining, and fun, but it is an entirely different game.

The reader will notice that this book is male-gender based. Many women enjoy archery as much as or more than men. It was just of convenience to write this with the masculine reference. The reader will also discover a West Coast bias. Not only because the author grew up as a westerner, but also because the West Coast has been a major setting for contemporary American archery. The upper Mid-West has played a significant role as well, and the author would like to make this recognition, too.

While this work is a comprehensive look into traditional archery, its past and present, it alone is not enough to "make an archer out of you." It is the individual's time and interest that will result in proficiency and develop into a love of this sport.

YOUNG BOWMEN

*Two kids on the warm, green, summer lawn, the sun bathing
the little towheaded boys. Carefully selected and dried
branches are strung with fishin' line and grasped in eager, little
hands. Cardboard box elephants, tigers, lions, and buffalo
adorn their game field. Like well practiced braves, the little boy
bowman and his trusted friend stalk and kill each target with
"genuine store-bought arrows."*

*"Come in, boys! Come in, boys! Your lunch is ready!"
mother implores from the door.*

*"Oh Mom, can't you see that there are dangerous beasts about,
and we need to slay them?"*

*"Boys, come in and eat your sandwiches and then spend the
rest of the afternoon hunting."*

*Sustained by their rations, the little bowman and his friend
long to find their way back out to the steaming jungles to hunt
crocodiles, leopards, and poisonous snakes. Dreams of adventure and fantasy course hotly through their souls. A little boy
lives in two worlds. One is the world of necessity, where he has
to deal with reality and dull routine. The other is the world of
ought-to-be, where the little bowman is freed to go into his
fanciful mind and put everything into its true proper order.*

*Beware, little bowman! Time will rob you of your world of
ought-to-be. Go back outside with your pal now and hunt the
swamps, plains, and jungles and slay those vicious beasts that
prowl your warm, green, summer lawn.*

Section I

EQUIPMENT

Check out Arnold O. Haugen's bow and clothing in the 1950's.

Chapter 1

PONDERING ABOUT BOWS

Sometimes I sit and muse about Ishi, the last native American raised in a pure Indian culture. He was a true archer. By this I mean that he loved the bow and lived the bow. He had very definite ideas on what constituted a good bow. His ideas and my ideas on this subject may differ, as might yours also. But, which one of us is right? Between Ishi, you, and I, we are all correct for our own purposes. I have long ago learned that the fountain of all bow knowledge is not contained in any one individual. In fact, we do well to glean just a small morsel of bow truth. Nevertheless, I have found myself at various times expounding to any with a willing ear, my garble on what constitutes a "proper bow."

Ask me at the end of a long, tiring week of bow making what the ideal bow is and I'll probably say it is a bow that is boxed and ready for shipment. Ask me at a moment of reverie and I'll say it was my first Eicholtz composite bow I bought as a youth. At a time of creativity, I'll say it's the new longbow I am working on. When I'm target shooting I'll say it is a long, light, accurate bow. Ask me when I'm hunting and I'll say it is my beat up old stable longbow. I, like most all archers, have many ideal bows. Frequently, bowmen buy or make many bows over time. With each bow comes a new wrinkle or new ideal. This is just the way it is. I have a recurve bow in my den that has been the undoing of several deer. I used it in the 1960's. At the time I felt that this bow was the ultimate in causing venison carnage. I pick it up now and wonder how I ever shot the thing. Yes, time and new ideas and concepts change one's thoughts about bows.

I do not wish this writing to be a long dissertation on the bow. My objective is to present information to give basic understanding to people new in the sport and further understanding to those who are well acquainted with the sport. I do it with the credentials of one who has spent a lifetime studying, making, and shooting all types of bows.

Back in the 1950's Ben Pearson was making thousands of hickory bows. These bows were almost indestructible as well as inexpensive. I had one which served me well in the rabbit patch. During the summer it was my almost-constant companion. I also used lemonwood and yew bows. With them I killed all sorts of small game—rabbits, doves, squirrels, possums, and quail. Then one day I shot a laminated composite bow and fell in love. It was smooth, very quick, accurate, and with little hand shock! I had to have one; but being only 15 years of age, funds were limited. So I would haunt Frank Eicholtz's archery shop and drool over his stock of bows. One was perfect. It was a laminated composite longbow that Howard Hill patterned his bows after. This 66" maple cored bow was 40 pounds at my draw. It had woven brown glass on the back and white unidirectional glass on the belly. There was no arrow rest, just a piece of leather. The price? $27.50—a small fortune in those days! I knew that my dad would be a hard nut to crack, so I went to work on my mother.

"Christmas is coming, Mom, and the only thing I want is a laminated bow."

"How much is it?"

"$27.50 plus tax."

"What? That's a lot of money! I don't think I can do it."

I was crushed. I never hounded my parents for things, so I figured it was a lost cause. A few days before Christmas, my mother took me aside and said, "I've squirreled some money together. Here, take this and go and buy your bow." Oh, did I ever love my mother!

The new Eicholtz bow launched me into a lifelong love of the laminated composite bow. There are several advantages to laminated construction. The biggest advantage, as I see it, is that they are much more durable. Breakage occurs less often than with the all wood bow. When the dyed-in-the-wool archers of the 1940's discovered the new way of making bows with fiberglass laminates, most of them forsook their wooden bows for the new durable composites.

18

Another advantage to the composite bow is that function can rule over form. The laminated composite construction allows the bowyer to freely experiment with an infinite variety of limb and handle riser styles. When a design is chosen, the bowyer can duplicate each bow precisely. This is not so with the wooden bow. The wooden bow has to pretty much follow the form of the stave, therefore, function may suffer. Each wooden bow has its own special character which can be very desirable or a demon. Every wooden-bow bowyer will tell you that they can have almost two identical staves, and for some unknown reason, one will produce a charming bow and the other a monster. This is especially true with yew wood, whereas, osage is more consistent. There are two things to be gleaned from this: you can find many diverse styles of laminated bows that shoot good (if they are made by experienced, clever bowyers), and if you get a wooden bow that is well made and shoots good, you have a very unique weapon that is an enchanting, pleasing delight which should be saved and cared for.

There are bowyers who are mechanics when it comes to laminated bows. They make well-constructed, good-shooting bows— often times made quickly and in large volume. Then there are bowyers who are artists. Because of the freedom of design allowed by laminated construction, artist bowyers marry form and function into sculptured, breathtakingly splendid weapons. The first bows I saw of this type were made by Harry Drake around 1954.

The 1950's and 60's produced many artistic bows which include those by Corkie Johnson, Harold Groves, FASCO, Damon Howatt, Custom Bow, Joe Fries, Sanders, Smithwick, Hit, Jack Howard, Dick Green, Perry, El Lobo, Tarbell, and others.

Some people claim that laminated construction makes a bow of quicker cast. This is not altogether true. I have witnessed wooden longbows that cast heavy arrows farther than composite recurves and longbows of similar draw weight. The thinner limbs on some laminated bows load down very readily with heavy shafts and lose efficiency—especially the short-limbed recurves.

Some bow types or styles lend themselves to certain functions better that others. Long recurves with weighted handle

19

risers, for example, are much better for target shooting than longbows—either composite or wood. Light handle-risered bows with long limbs are better for the quick-shooting, instinctive, hunting archer. Recurve bows are smoother and often quicker than straight-end bows, but they may be more sensitive to errors in shooting form. Laminated and wooden longbows tend to kick more and be more unpleasant to shoot.

I believe that if a person is a very deliberate shooter, with a solid draw, anchor, and aim (basically interested in hunting and field archery), a moderate length recurve would be a good bow for him.

The laminated longbow has really grown in popularity in the last 10 years. In fact, it is more popular now than it ever has been. The reason for this is not because it is a superior weapon, but because it is simple and effective. Under hunting conditions, the laminated longbow lends itself strongly to the task. Good ones are very forgiving to inconsistencies in shooting form. (Isn't that the natural mode of the hunter?) Their light weight offers a comfortable weapon that packs easily through brush or over mountain crest. Another reason for their popularity is that they offer a radical departure from complicated weapons. A number of us get real tired of our modern, high-tech lives, and the longbow allows us a chance to return to the simple basics.

Some people want to become very basic in their approach to archery. They choose the self-wood longbow. These bows adapt themselves especially well to people who enjoy making their own equipment and to those who are well seasoned in the sport. One has to continually fuss over his equipment if he chooses to go the self-wood bow route. This fussing is what the fun is all about to any enamored with this part of the game. Fortunately for the newcomer, there are now several fine books on self-wood bows available to reference.

Another even more basic branch of traditional archery is what some call "primitive archery." In this the bows and arrows are constructed using the most basic tools and materials, often copying the equipment used by aboriginal people. Participants in primitive archery are growing in number and are often cultish in their zeal. I personally don't indulge in primitive archery, except in conversation, but enjoy watching the fun.

When you buy your next bow, remember that just because a company makes lots of them, doesn't necessarily mean they make them good. Bows are a lot like automobiles: the finest ones seem to come from the smaller companies. Humans are very susceptible to advertising and commercialism, therefore, make intelligent decisions in your selection process. The best way to do this is to try several makes of bows and talk to their owners. Going to archery shoots and events is helpful in the selection process.

When I look over a bow for quality, I usually start at the nocks. Believe it or not, it is difficult to shape a nock. It requires learned skill, and there is no way to hurry the process without it manifesting itself. The nock overlay, if used, should be symmetrically cut. Nowhere should you find file marks, roughness, or sharp edges.

Eyeballing the finish is my next inspection. A good finish should be void of bubbles, runs, splotches, or other blemishes. Most inexperienced bowmakers do not apply good finishes. It takes a great deal of sophistication to put a decent finish on a bow. Therefore be aware that if the bow is poorly finished, it may be that the bowmaker is deficient in other areas too. Bow companies do not put great finishes on poorly crafted bows. Consequently, if a bow has a nice finish, it probably has good craftsmanship as well.

Quality bows do not have marks left in by power machinery or hand tools. Check the side of the limbs on the wood core for sander marks and inspect the area around the arrow rest for scratches. If the bow has handle overlays (wood or other materials glued on top of the fiberglass), check to see that they feather out smoothly and with symmetry. A master bowyer is very fussy about symmetry.

I always check for limb alignment. A good bow's limbs will not twist as they are being drawn. Sight down the string, it should be centered down the middle of the limb from tip to tip. Also, check a recurve bow's string grooves to see that they are centered and not crooked.

The length of bow that one chooses is a fundamental key of good shooting. You will hear many opinions concerning what constitutes the best length; but let me give you something more than opinion. Then let me relate my personal beliefs.

Longer bows tend to be less sensitive to shooting inconsistencies. This is because the limbs of a longer bow do not travel at the tips as far as a shorter bow's do, as the archer is coming to a full draw. If the archer is a bit inconsistent in his draw length, the limbs on the shorter bow will have a greater travel variance during this inconsistency than those of the longer bow's limbs. This travel variance really can affect limb recovery speed, causing the archer to shoot primarily high or low. It secondarily may affect arrow spine strength, thereby causing left or right arrow placement. Thus the draw-length error is magnified by the shorter bow.

The angle of the bowstring from a longer bow at full draw is less than one from a shorter bow. The greater the angle, the harder it is for the archer to get a clean, smooth release from his drawing fingers. Heavy bows make the archer even more susceptible to this phenomenon. Critical string angles tend to squash the drawing fingers together, causing improper pressure on the arrow nock. Consequently, the archer may have difficulty with porpoising arrows. This is especially bad with broadhead points, because it leads to windplaning.

A number of archers stay away from short bows. They recognize that they are a curse to accuracy. The great Howard Hill was one of them. In traditional archery today, you will notice a host of shooters who feel the same way. I have always been an advocate of longer bows. This is because I've shot enough tournament archery to know that fine accuracy was never achieved by short bows. The master bowyer, Frank Eicholtz, was a very short man with a 26-inch arrow draw. He preferred to shoot 69-inch or longer bows. He even claimed that longer bows were quicker because the length of their limbs supplied greater mechanical advantage and vibrated (recovered) quicker. Remember, short bows have short levers and long bows have long levers. Therefore, long bows have greater mechanical advantage or leverage. This is very simplistic, but it is worth noting.

Short bows are advantageous for archers shooting from a confined stand, where clearance and movement are restricted.

Horseback shooting and canoe shooting are better with the short bow. I venture to say that a great number of short-bow users are more enamored of the way a short bow looks and feels than by its accuracy.

I personally prefer bows between 66 and 70 inches with my 28-inch draw length. Longbows get shorter immediately when being drawn, and recurves tend to maintain their length because of the recurve section opening up. Therefore, I believe that recurves can be a touch shorter than straight-end bows. At any rate, my advice to others is to always stay on the longer side when choosing bow length.

A section on bows wouldn't be complete without a discussion on the classic American style longbow. These bows have been around since the early 1950's. As mentioned in other parts of this book, they were popularized by Howard Hill. The American style longbow is a straight-end bow of composite construction. They are generally 65 to 72 inches in length and incorporate very short handle riser sections—whether reversed or standard, it makes no difference. The limbs are usually reflexed, but the deflex-reflex style is acceptable. The core wood can be any species. The limbs of these bows are very narrow, and their cores are deep (thick).

The American style longbow is a simple bow. It is also an esthetically pleasing bow to look upon. It requires a lot of human input to shoot. It is a very effective hunting weapon, and quite enjoyable to use. Because of these characteristics, there has been a devoted number of hardcore American-longbow shooters for over 40 years. I have come to believe that it takes about one year of earnest practice to become good with them. The effort is worthwhile, because I know a legion of archers who swear that their success afield is greater with the American style longbow than with any other style bow.

On today's market there are a number of composite longbow styles appearing that do not fit the mold of the American style. Some are short, some have wide limbs, and some have extra long handle risers with highly deflexed-reflexed limbs. There is nothing inferior about these styles, but they do not function the same as the classic version.

The complete traditional archer has many functional bows at his command. If one dabbles in the sport, one or two bows will suffice. But if archery is your game, you should have many bows.

Most of us have a bow or two around that is used for very adverse conditions. I have an old bow that I made 25 years ago for such purposes. I use it mainly for carp shooting. I have painted it with a tough black paint so it won't show its abuses. In the course of a year, it will be thrown on the ground, dunked in the water, and dragged over the rocks. I have a similar bow made for the express purpose of hunting goats in rocky alpine terrain.

Many archers who spend a lot of time hunting from tree stands, prefer to have a shorter bow for this purpose. This type of bow can be made with slower and less sensitive limbs because the overall shooting distance will not be great. On the other hand, one of my archery friends does a lot of elk hunting in fairly open country. Longer shots are the rule, and he prefers quick shooting, heavy bows in the 70-plus-pound class.

A fellow was telling me some time ago that a bow with white glass was useless for hunting. He reasoned that, in the woods, the white glass would show up and spook game. This is partly true. However, in a lot of places where I hunt there is snow on the ground. A white glassed bow is perfect under these conditions. One who often hunts in the snow should consider a bow of this type.

Every complete archer will have a light draw-weight bow. Bows in the 40-pound range, for most people, are excellent for practicing. Many arrows can be shot without the fatigue and consequential loss of shooting form that heavier bows inflict upon us.

Muscles need warming up before being taxed. Lighter bows are perfect for this. Most of us will have periods of non-shooting. It only takes a couple of weeks for our muscles to start loosing their tone. What better way to restart a season than with a lighter bow?

As we grow older, our muscles, joints, and bones tend to suffer the rigors of aging. Reasonable care should be given. It is just not wise to start out on a day's shooting with a 60-plus-pound bow with tendonitis in the shoulder or elbow.

A 45-pound bow is efficient and will cast well-matched arrows at good speeds. The archer can often get by with 5/16" diameter wood arrow shafting—which makes for good matching. With carefully selected broadheads a 45-pound bow will easily dispatch deer-sized animals at moderate distances.

Some people say that lighter bows don't shoot flat enough and therefore are not as accurate. With properly matched arrows, this argument is weak. Others say that heavy bows make for cleaner string releases. This is a strong argument for learning to shoot a 45-pound bow. When you learn to get a clean release from the 45-pound bow, your release with the heavy bow will be even better.

From my experience, I have found that bows from about 55 to 60 pounds should be in everyone's working collection. This weight range offers the optimum efficiency for most bows. That is, for the amount of energy the archer puts into it, he receives the most returns in arrow speed, etc. A man of average size and strength will have no problem handling a 55-pound bow. Wood arrow shafts are readily available for this spine. A bow of this weight is adequate for most North American game. If an archer can afford, or desires to own, only one or two bows, I would highly recommend a bow of about 55 pounds.

I know lots of traditional archers. For the most part, they generally do most of their hunting with bows from 60 to 80 pounds. These weights call for constant practice by the bowman in order to maintain adequate strength for proper handling. There is no need to fear that you do not have enough potential power to kill most any game animal. These bows will zip arrows through moose, elk, even grizzly bears. Speaking in general terms, they are not good to take out for extended shooting periods, because they will wear a person out. Bows of this weight range are the mainstay hunting weapons for most traditional bowmen.

Some of us have or use bows that draw in excess of 80 pounds. In my younger days, before I critically broke my left shoulder, I enjoyed shooting these heavy weights. Believe me, they shouldn't be considered in your arsenal unless you give serious attention to the ramifications of shooting them. Bows over 80 pounds are only functional in the hands of bowmen who properly condition their bodies and minds to the stresses involved in drawing them. It is unwise for someone who is unskilled in the use of such powerful weapons to try to pull one to full draw to prove that he can do it. We all, at sometime, fall into this trap. As a result, I've seen many who have hurt themselves with such injuries as strained or torn ligaments and muscles in the hands, fingers, elbows, and shoulders.

Another bow type that often surfaces in our arsenals is what I call the "ego" or "wow" bow. This is the bow that is a work of art. Not only do we have these to please ourselves, we use them to wow others. Some of us, who are inflicted with the disease called pride, are susceptible to owning an ego bow or two. When we gather at a big archery shoot, our wow bows are used instead of our practical, simple weapons. The bad thing about this type bow is that, like any other highly crafted article, it is costly. One archer told me that by using his wow bow, it was his way of making a statement about himself as an archer. (Personally, I think it is just a way for us big kids to show off.)

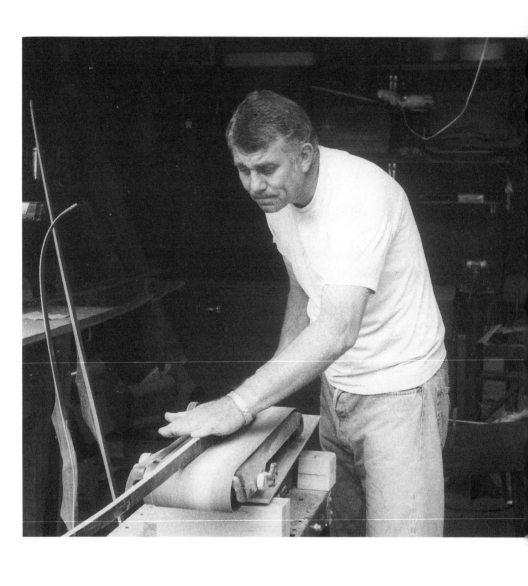

Chapter 2
THE BOWYER

Prime yew staves were a dime a dozen in the early 1950's because the whole archery world was being smitten by the composite bow. My older brother, Lee, spent some time in Oregon and northern California, and he brought me a dozen or so yew staves. I really appreciated this, because money was hard to come by for a young teenager. I made several bows from these staves. My next effort was a 60-inch, 60-pound, straight-end composite bow. It had woven fiberglass on the back and plastic on the belly.

Southern California had several fine bowyers. I would visit as many as possible, and receive advice and instruction.

When 19 years of age, I went into the Air Force for four years. Still hopelessly smitten with archery, I continued making bows for myself.

1963 found me working for a company called Seattle Archery in El Cajon, California. At this plant, we made a line of bows called "FASCO." Later on, we moved the plant to Washington state. During the seven years I worked there we made thousands of bows. Besides the "FASCO" line of bows, we also made Drake, Eicholtz, Morris, Thompson, and Root bows. Believe me, it got to be tiring work. When I left the company in 1970 to become a school teacher, I made a secret resolve not to get into mass bow manufacturing for a long while.

From 1970 to 1982, I made bows for local trade only. Then, in 1982, I seriously started crafting bows under the name of "Cascade Mountain Archery." I chose the name because of my affinity for these mountains. I have spent years hunting in them, and they hold a special charm for me.

There are many people now who want to go into bow-making to earn a living. I think that I am qualified to talk about this. First of all, let's discuss money. If a person thinks that he can make a great gob of money by making bows, then he'd better think again. I know of very few who ever do more than scratch out a living. Some people like the excitement of being a bow maker. It keeps them in the spotlight. It feeds their egos. Others go into bow-making because they truly love to make bows. But this grows old in a hurry, because bow-making is hard work.

As for me, I've probably succumbed to all these reasons. I've made a living out of it, but I've never become monetarily rich. I like being a bowyer because I feel I'm really connected to the sport. My ego soars when someone tells me that they love my bows. Finally, I like the creative experience of making bows. It is sort of like a drug to me. If I go very long without building a bow, I get very restless.

I would like to relate what being a bowyer is like from my personal perspective. I will refer to three classes of bow makers: (1) the bowmaker, (2) the bowyer, and (3) the master bowyer. The bowmaker is the person who makes an occasional bow or is apprenticing with a professional shop. Anyone who has been bow-making less than four years and hasn't made a couple of hundred bows is certainly not a bowyer. A bowyer is a professional bowmaker that has made a number of different styles of bows. The bowyer is an archer. He has a good understanding of the sport and its history. A master bowyer is a person who clearly excels in bow making. Not only do his bows excel, but they are often works of art. To reach this level, a person has to be a proven bowyer for at least eight years, or so, and have national recognition of his talents. In America today, they would be people like Harry Drake, Tim Meigs, Larry Hatfield, Bill Stewart, Harold Groves, and Jack Howard. These people have paid their dues.

At a recent shoot, an egotistic, budding bowmaker was going from one booth to another talking to the various bowmakers about their bows. He had done a lot of research in Nagler, Hickman, and Klopsteg. He was a bit brash about his criticisms of everyone's bows. He looked over my bows and tried to engage me in a conversation about their neutral axis. I'm afraid I wasn't to responsive. Later, he had the audacity to try telling Larry Hatfield, the plant manager of Howatt bows, how to make a better bow. He explained to Larry something about his own revolutionary new ideas in bow making. Larry looked at him in astonishment and said that bowmakers had been doing those things for years! Maybe when this fellow has grown in years and wisdom and puts in his dues, he may have something to say.

The bowyer in a large shop is like any journeyman in a profession. He may have many roles during the workday. Layup and gluing, limb-shaping and aligning, handle- riser shaping, sanding and finishing, and supervision and training may be what his daily routine consists of. Never does he take a production bow through all of its operations by himself. A large shop bowyer quite often is engaged in repetitive routine work. I used to feel real satisfaction in getting out a record number of bows in the shortest possible time and still maintaining high quality.

The small shop bowyer seems to get more satisfaction from bow-making because he is involved with making the complete bow. He has more decision-making opportunities. Let me give a typical routine at my shop. Early in the morning I go into the shop and light up the heaters. Later, I go back in and hope it is warm. I take a bow that was glued the previous day out of its form. The limbs are scribed and cut out, and the bow is rough-sanded and weighed. Another bow has to be laid up and glued next. By this time, the shop is warm and my feet are starting to hurt. A phone call comes in from some guy wanting to know when his bow will be ready. (I have already told him three times when to expect it.) Gluing is usually a messy job, and when the next bow is glued, I wash up and grab a quick bite to eat. Next, it's time to align and shape a bow. These steps are hard work and may take a couple of hours. By now, my legs and feet are really tired, and I am wearing a mantle of wood and fiberglass dust. My wife calls to ask when I'll be in for dinner. I want to tell her right away, but I really need to spray one bow that has to be shipped next week. So I spend an hour spraying the bow. Finally, I go over to the compressor and blow the dust off my clothes and turn off all the power and go into the house. My wife asks if I'd like to go to the movies. All I want to do is go to bed. She is sympathetic and tells to me to go and shower and she'll get my dinner. I eat and go to bed. The next morning I get up early, light my shop heaters, and ...

Let me not let the reader think that bow-making is not enjoyable. Often it can be outright exciting. "What if" are the two words that make up excitement and bring out thought and creativity. I was sitting in church one Sunday listening to the speaker—or I should say trying to listen, because he was very dull. My mind kept thinking of how wood might be laminated to form a pattern that would look unique under clear glass. I fairly twitched with excitement. Now, on Sunday I should be looking for religious inspiration not bow-making inspiration. "What if I cut this piece of wood this way," I thought to myself. The next day, I was out in the shop working on my "what ifs." The more "what ifs" a bowyer works on, the better he becomes.

Being artistic is a virtue for anyone wanting to make bows. The traditional bow is an esthetic weapon as well as a functional one. Form and function often clash in the making of bows. Some bows are made for function only, and boy can they get to be ugly. Conversely, some are so pretty it is a shame to take them out to shoot. A real master bowyer can marry form and function in the most marvelous ways.

Of the two, function is the easiest to get right. On the market, you'll find many bows that shoot good, but finding a good-looking bow is harder. When I talk to other bowyers, I'm frequently amused by their lack of knowledge of the artistic dimensions. I would recommend that the aspiring bowmaker take a basic art course. This might help him understand line and form, color and value, texture and pattern, harmony and contrast, and more.

One has to be very philosophical about bow making. For the 40-odd years I've been doing it, I have seen countless numbers of men go into it (I have never met a female bowmaker). Most seldom stay at it. Their sojourn may be a year or two. Few make it to ten years, and only a handful will do twenty years or more. Like most things in life, bowmakers and bows are very soon forgotten. I guess, in the great scheme of things, they are not too important.

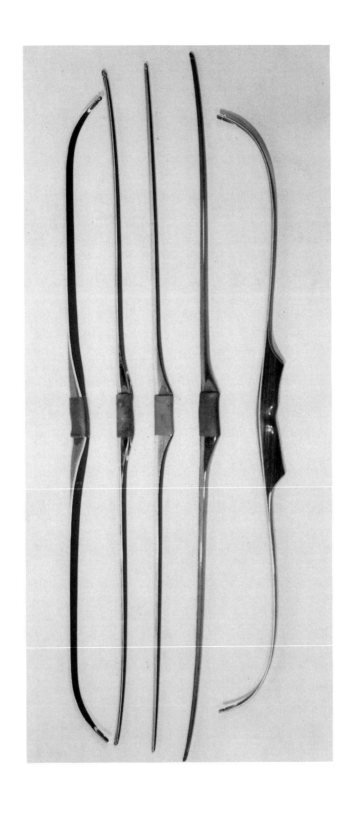

Chapter 3

YEW AND ME or,

Taxus brevifola and Homo jackasarcherus

I recall when laminated composite bows became popular. Self-wood bows turned into unwanted commodities. Around 1954 it was possible to buy very nice yew bows for as little a five dollars apiece. As you know, a quality yew bow now costs several hundred dollars, and it is great fun to shoot.

I had a friend Bill, back then, who was a college student and an avid archer. He was the proud owner of a 72-inch yew longbow, handmade by the grand old man of yew wood, Earl Ullrich. My friend really liked this bow, but temptation enticed him to order a 70-pound, 58-inch recurve. He called me when the bow arrived, and we immediately took off for the field range. Both of us were amazed at the speed of this little bow. It appeared to shoot absolutely flat on the 55-yard target, and it was right on, on the 80-yarder.

That evening, we took the new composite and the old yew bow over to the golf course to try some comparisons by flight shooting. Our arrows were heavy, compressed cedar "Forgewoods." Bill pulled the reflexed recurve bow to the limit and proceeded to shoot six red-nocked arrows down the fairway. They seemed to travel extremely fast. Next, he shot six black-nocked arrows from the yew longbow; they seemed to go fast, too. We trekked down the fairway to retrieve the missiles. There were two groups. One group was 20 yards beyond the other. To our surprise, the first group had red nocks!. The yew longbow out shot the short, recurve composite by a full 20 yards! This didn't seem congruous, so we turned around and shot in the other direction. This time, the black-nocked arrows were shot from the composite, the results were the same, the longbow still had quicker cast.

With a little reasoning, we could tell that the heavier limbed longbow would push the 650-grain arrows with more authority.

Long, heavy limbs not only handle heavy arrows well, they also are less sensitive to shooting errors. Herein is a lesson that one may apply effectively in choosing hunting equipment. There is a growing number of composite longbows on the market with extra long handle-risers and short limbs. These bows sail lighter weight arrows quickly, but they don't do so well with heavy shafts, and they definitely are more sensitive to mistakes in shooting form under hunting conditions.

For the last few centuries, archers have held a special reverence for yew wood. Often referred to as the wood given by the gods to the archer, it has played a significant part in our sport. The sapwood and heartwood mechanically work effectively together to produce a springy weapon of utmost delight. The unique, honey color appeals to the eye.

Yew trees are scattered over the Pacific Northwest. They usually grow singularly. They are small trees, from 20 to 50 feet tall, and one to one and a half feet in diameter. They tend to be full of limbs and poorly formed. The best ones generally grow in the Cascade Range of Washington, Oregon, and northern California. Although the trees grow at elevations ranging from sea level to 8000 ft., the best bow timber comes from 1000 to 3000 feet. The lowland yew grows too fast and is not strong enough. Yew from over 3000 feet is often too small, bushy, and full of knots, therefore not suitable for stave material.

The yew tree did not have much commercial value until the late 1980's, when it was discovered that the bark could be processed into the medical cancer treatment "Taxol." Since then, thousands have been logged for their bark. This really disturbed me until a year ago. My sister-in-law had her cancer arrested from the "Taxol" medicine, and now I have another reason to like the yew. Luckily, the "Taxol" can now be procured from nursery stock trees.

Yew trees often do strange things to people. I know more than a few people, who, with passion, actively search for these trees in order to find bow material. I was hunting with this fellow once on his private deer hunting grounds. We were quietly stalking along a trail when my friend suddenly became very intense. From his actions, I could tell he had spotted something. He pointed up ahead about 30 yards. I looked where he indicated but couldn't see anything. He intently pointed again. For the life of me, I couldn't see the deer. He started walking slowly forward, and I followed. The fellow pointed again at something in the bushes. Finally, I whispered, "I can't see anything. Where is it?" He grinned and pointed at a yew tree stuck in among the firs.

"Isn't that a grand tree?" he asked.

"You mean it was a tree I was stalking?" I replied in disgust. For the rest of the day, my friend was more intent on showing yew trees than finding game.

I became acquainted with the great master of yew wood, Earl Ullrich, in the 1960's. Earl spent a lifetime logging yew in Oregon for archery purposes. He was active in his obsession with this tree right up until his death while in his 90's. Our bow shop received a number of laminations from him around 1968. By the 1970's, I was personally ordering yew from him, and he wanted me to build bows for his shop. I was over-extended at the time and declined. We had lots of correspondence over the years. His unique penmanship was something to behold.

In 1982, I started making a highly crafted, laminated longbow line which was dubbed the "Diamondback." I still make it. I put rattlesnake skin on the backs of these bows. I believe I was the first person to do this commercially. These bows became very popular in my bow line. While working in the shop one day, I happened across some extra choice, high elevation, yew lams that I had been saving. These lams were cut in 1948 by Ullrich. I decided to make myself a "Diamondback" bow using Earl's laminations. I, like so many other bowmakers, rarely make myself a bow, so I decided it would be one that I could use on targets as well as hunting. This bow turned out exceptionally nice. It was 59 pounds at my draw and 68 inches in length. I applied an eastern diamondback rattler skin on the back. The belly was covered with clear glass to show off Earl's brilliant, honey colored, tight grained, yew laminations. Bright red amaranth set off the handle riser.

As a school teacher I am often involved with fifth- and sixth-graders at outdoor school camp. For a week one September, I taught archery classes. For part of each session, I would put on a shooting demonstration. Aerial shooting was a portion of it. During the spare times, I would have the kids toss up disks for me to shoot. They loved to see arrows hitting the high flying disks. By the end of the week, I was getting pretty good! (At least I thought so.)

By Friday, I was getting restless to return home. Deer season had just started that week, and I was anxious to get out. Saturday was a workday in the shop. Late that afternoon, I couldn't stand it any longer. I grabbed my bow and quiver and headed to a large island in southern Puget Sound which is near my home. My hunting bow was the same yew bow used at school camp.

Just before dusk, I spotted two deer on an old logging track. Both animals were does, and one was extremely large. The big one jumped into a thickly covered area of trees and brush, and I followed. I climbed a small mound near where the deer disappeared to get a better look into the trees. With a nocked arrow, I scanned intently. There was a crashing sound to my left, and a deer was bounding swiftly through the trees leading to my right. Automatically, I raised and drew my bow. The hours spent shooting moving targets earlier in the week had me in tune. I released the arrow as the animal was about 30 yards away and going full steam. The arrow and deer both went through a bush. There was that recognizable thud, as steel hits flesh, and the deer went wildly crashing through the forest.

I waited a few minutes and went to investigate for a blood trail. I couldn't find anything! Darkness was rapidly descending, and my vision was getting worse. I had to go get a flashlight. When I got back with the light, the woods were pitch black.

Even though I didn't see the arrow hit the deer, I knew my shot was accurate. For over an hour, I carefully searched the area for sign. Finally, my light beam revealed a shiny, crimson droplet on a leaf. This clue led me to more signs, and the deer was found. Remarkably, the arrow was still intact, sticking out behind her ribs. The broadhead had ranged forward into the chest cavity.

The deer was huge for a blacktail doe. Later, upon tooth examination, it was determined that she was 13 years old. Even though aged by deer standards, her meat was very tasty.

I have often reflected back to my adventure of that evening hunt, and especially the instinctive shot made with my yew cored longbow. But another chapter of the hunt occurred much later. A good friend of mine was over the following summer for some stump shooting. He wanted see the island where I hunted deer, and I took him there. We came to the spot where my deer had died. I again recounted the tale of the hunt—probably for the tenth time. He looked around and said, "Do you notice something unusual about this place?" I couldn't see anything out of the ordinary, so he pointed to a perfectly shaped old yew tree that stood over the place where my deer had fallen. I have since looked for other yew trees on the island without much luck. Maybe old Earl Ullrich was trying to say something to me. I don't know.

Ah, but this story is not yet over. A fellow from Seattle dropped by and ordered a longbow from me one day. We got talking, and low and behold, he was the owner of the property that I hunted. When he received his longbow, he was so pleased with it, that he gave me the yew tree. I had desires to reverently cut this tree down and make another bow and maybe give a stack of laminations to some young bowmaker who would understand the significance of this wood. What a fitting end to the story that would be. But I've since decided to just let the tree stand.

From time to time, I go over to the island and stand under my tree's branches and bask in pleasant memories.

Chapter 4
SOME BOW PROVERBS

Heavy Bow

In 1966, I went with three other bowmen to the rugged Olympic Mountains in far western Washington state for a deer and bear hunt. We hiked way back into the mountains and set up a camp in a splendid alpine valley. The first day out, another fellow and myself shared a kill on a young doe. We dressed and skinned and hung her in camp. We had her completely eaten in three days.

One of the chums had a 60-inch, 65-pound recurve bow produced by a leading, large manufacturer. He had killed an elk the previous season with it and was very proud of its power. The rest of us were shooting longer bows of lesser weight. In fact, this fellow was almost becoming obnoxious about how fast his bow was.

On the last day, as we were hiking out, we were subjected to his endless chatter. We came to a rare opening in the forest, and one of us ask him if he cared to prove how fast his bow was by seeing how far it could cast an arrow into the clearing. More than happy to demonstrate, he drew his fiberglass shaft to the head and let her rip. Way out across the clearing the arrow flew. It landed so far out near the far edge of the clearing, we could hardly see it. Wow! Yes, this was really everything he said—or was it? He then looked at me and challenged, "Fred, why don't you see what your bow will do?" And he handed me one of his arrows.

"Well, okay, if that's what you want," I reluctantly replied. Now I'll never hear the end of it, I thought. My bow was a new 66-inch, 53-pound recurve. It had a solid micarta handle riser. I also had been experimenting with putting a fiberglass strip across the riser and fading it out into the limb a few inches. I called this process fiberglass shimming. I knew that my bow was quick enough, but it was no match for a 65-pounder.

I took my stance while the fellows grinned at me. I pulled the arrow to the point and cast it off. The shaft shot out and out and well beyond the end of the clearing.

I couldn't believe the distance it went, and neither could the two other hooting fellows. But the chagrined challenger could say nothing. We found my arrow a full 40 yards beyond his.

The moral: Just because your bow is heavy doesn't necessarily mean that it is fast.

Hand-Over Bow

When my three friends and I arrived back at the car after our deer and bear hunt, we piled in and headed down the dusty, seldom used mountain road. Shortly, we came upon a large congregation of blue grouse by the side of the road. We all grabbed some arrows and bows and jumped out of the old sedan. Grouse make excellent table fare and sport, and we wanted to get a bunch. I quickly dispatched two fat ones and used up my blunt-tipped arrows. The car, with my spare arrows, was a hundred yards away. I spotted one of the fellows, Jerry, going to the sedan to replenish his arrow supply. I asked him to bring me some, too. He told me to hold his bow, and then he hustled off for more arrows.

I heard a noise in a fir tree above me, and there sat several big grouse tempting me. I glanced at the fine broadhead arrows in Jerry's bow quiver. They were his pride and joy. A wicked feeling came over me as I took one out and drew on the nearest grouse. I shot and missed; that arrow probably landed in the next county. Well, I sinned once, so I figured I might as well sin again. I aimed another broadhead at the second grouse. I shot, and came so close I clipped a feather. Well, two arrows lost, might as well shoot another, I thought, as I placed a third broadhead on the arrow shelf. Arrow number three sliced clean through the bird like butter. The grouse fluttered through the trees with me following. When it was secured, Jerry came up with the blunt-pointed arrows. He glanced at the bird in my hand then said, "Hey, I thought you were out of arrows." Then he spied the missing arrows in his quiver. I started to howl at his plight. Jerry was a great sport, and he grinned. He knew I pulled one over on him. He couldn't complain too much, though because I had given him his bow.

We rounded up all the dead birds and threw them into the car trunk. The last guy back was carrying a grouse. He didn't want to open the trunk so he put it under the front seat.

Merrily, we took off in a cloud of dust, heading down the mountain road to the highway. When we came to some steep hairpin turns all hell broke loose. Evidently, the grouse that was under the front seat was resurrected. Its wings roared into life and it flew straight to the back window. Reversing direction, it whirred right into the front windshield spreading feathers and blood and crap all over the shocked occupants. It committed mayhem on us for a minute or so until its neck was abruptly rung. It was a fun trip!

The moral: Before you hand your bow to some fool, remember that it might be returned in unexpected ways.

Fast Bow

The following spring I went out stump shooting with my 65-pound, recurve friend. The bow shop was making a 54-inch, super fast recurve called the "Drake Hunter-Flight," and it held the world's hand-held distance record at the time. I had just finished a 50-pounder for myself. I knew that I could accurately outshoot my friend most every time in the stump field; with this hot new bow, I could make his 65-pounder look bad. That day the little bow shot arrows very fast over, under, and on each side of the target. I couldn't hit a thing with it. My friend smiled most of the day.

The moral: Just because your bow is fast doesn't necessarily mean that it's accurate.

Champ Bow

When I was a teenager I bought a bow just like the national champion, ol' Rube, used. He could shoot the center out of the bull's-eye on any target from coast to coast. I used this bow a long time and became pretty good with it, even though it had an unforgiving nature. After all, the champ used one just like it. One day I used another brand. My scores leaped up.

The moral: Just because the champ uses it doesn't necessarily mean it will work for you.

Fad Bow

A long-time longbow shooter friend of mine went into a large archery shop about a score of years ago to inquire about purchasing a new longbow. "You don't want one of those!" said the owner. "They're no good. This is what you really need," he said, pointing to a rack of compounds. Go into this shop today and the owner will say, "Here, buy one of these longbows. They're real archery."

The moral: One who sells you the bow may be selling the latest fad for profit.

Assessment Bow

I had a booth at a recent traditional archery shoot. One fellow stopped by and we talked bows for awhile. He related that he had made his own bow and would like my opinion of it. I said, "Sure, go get it." A shop owner friend of mine was helping me with my booth when this fellow returned with his homemade recurve. He handed it to me for inspection, and I eyeballed it. The bow was a bit crude but not bad for a beginner. I could tell by his anxious face that he eagerly awaited my judgment. "Well, what do you think?" he queried. My friend at the booth, an excellent judge of bows, was surprised at my answer. To him the bow was a club, but I said in reply that I thought it was a great bow. I meant what I said. You see, I have a weakness for all bows, especially if they are homemade. The fellow was pleased with my positive assessment, and he walked happily away.

My friend said, "Fred, that was an awful bow. How come you said you liked it?"

"Well," I replied, "you see, I never met a bow that I didn't like."

The moral: Assessing a bow is like assessing a person, you should try to see it through the eyes of its creator.

Ram-Bow

A very popular activity for 16-year-olds, in my era, was the "goose." I'm not talking about the bird, but the jab in the butt. I had several archery pals my age back then. We had discovered that a bow tip made an excellent "gooser," especially a recurve bow tip, because its form naturally lent itself to the application. There was a great field archery range in the park called "Gold Gulch." The course wound its way up, down, around, and through a wonderful eucalyptus forest. My chums and I would administer a good goose if one of us was plodding up a hill to the next target too slowly. I tell you, we had to really step lively and avoid walking single file at all times to prevent our rear ends from being explored by a bow-nock. I am sorry to say that I reveled in being a "gooser." (Being a "goosee" was not pleasant.)

Occasionally, one of us would let our guard down, and you could hear a voice wail out across the park, "Whoo-whoo-hee-hee-owhie!" We all had our own individual screams when being jabbed. Sometimes, when I'd arrive at the range late, I would sit and listen. After a bit, I'd hear "Ha-Ha-Oh-Oh-Yeow!!" and I would immediately know that Ray just took an incoming up by target seven. Then, I would just head up in that direction and find the chums. As disgusting as this custom seems, we would all indulge in it. 16-year-old boys do disgusting things, you know.

All of this came back to haunt me one day. The monthly club shoot is what did it. It was a marvelous, sunny morning. I was assigned to a foursome of an attractive young woman, her husband, and one of my chums. We proceeded through a few targets on the course. Target number six was a 55-yarder across a canyon. We all shot it and headed across the canyon to retrieve our missiles. The echelon paraded single file up the hill toward the target with the lady in front wearing tight gray slacks, me second, and the others following. My mind was in its usual fogged-out condition. The lady was slowly plodding along, and what a dandy behind she had! Without much conscious thought, I instinctively gave an ample ram where I imagined the bull's-eye to be with the upper nock of my "Drake" bow. (This is what is referred to in archery as "instinctive shooting.") She uttered out a "Wee-Wee-Oohh" sound that I didn't recognize. This brought me to my senses. Oh, my gosh! What had I done? Her husband grabbed my shoulder and twirled me around. He was saying words to me through clinched teeth. I knew I was a goner and deserving of any punishment he would mete out. My chum was smiling like a magpie on a fresh cow-pie. The lady's husband relaxed his grip on my shoulder and started to grin and then laugh. He could see some humor in my plight. Being a boy once himself, he let me go with a stern warning.

A funny thing about this episode was that whenever I would see the attractive lady after that, she would have a sparkle in her eye and give me a devilish smile—now I wonder what that was all about!

The moral: Before you instinctively shoot your bow at a tantalizing target, make sure you know the ram-ifications of your shot.

Skunk Bow: The Three Contestant Shoot-Off

Laughter and noise erupted that mid-1960's fall evening from the Ox Bow. Inside, 15 to 20 bow benders where enjoying the opportunity to warm up and rehash the happenings of the day's hunt. Decorating the walls and ceiling were dozens and dozens of arrows, each donated by some bow hunter in the past. Yes, Fred Bear had one there, too. In one corner of the tavern gushed a lively conversation from two friends, Mike and Jack. It was obvious that they had had several mugs of the golden brew. Both Mike and Jack were marvelous shots, and upon occasions like this, were trying to convince one another just how marvelous they really were. "I can outshoot you any day of the week!" Mike was saying.

"Yeah!" Jack retorted. "What about last weekend's shoot?"

"That's different. I only got three hours sleep the night before."

"Excuses! Excuses! You've got more of them than Dr. Carter's got pills," Jack said.

"Alright, let's go outside right now, and I'll prove I'm better than you!" Mike challenged.

"Fine with me! Someone, set up a target!" Everyone piled outside to watch the fun. Jack stumbled and nearly fell over.

"You're nothing but a drunk," Mike said. "I don't want to take advantage of you."

"Don't worry about me. I could whip your behind if I was twice as drunk!" This got Mike even more. It was hard to tell which one had imbibed more.

A round, portable, commercial straw target was set up 20 yards away alongside the tavern. A paper plate served as a bull's-eye. Mike motioned for Jack to shoot first. Jack was happy to oblige. A portly man in his late twenties, he raised his recurve. The glaze on his eyes quickly vanished. With a deliberate draw and anchor, he shot his arrow into the center of the plate. The observers clapped with glee, and Jack grinned like a possum with a persimmon.

Mike was a wiry man in his mid-thirties. He was tough as nails. Not concerned at all with Jack's shot, he cast his own arrow next to it. A roar of delight sprang forth. Mike repeated again with another arrow in the center. By this time, the onlookers were going from amused to amazed. Jack countered with two more in the center. This went on until there was a dozen shafts in the paper plate. Truly a remarkable demonstration under the circumstances. Finally Mike said, "This target stuff is too easy. Let's prove this on some live game."

Jack agreed.

Stars graced the alpine heavens as the boys put their bows and arrows in the bed of the pick-up. They jumped into the cab and headed down the dark, pine-lined, mountain road. After a few miles, near an old dump-site, the boys spotted two small, red eyes glowing in their headlights. They slammed on the brakes and piled out, grabbing their bows. Both Jack and Mike went charging off toward the eyes, anxious to get in the first shot. They stopped simultaneously and drew and shot.

"I got 'im one yelled."

"No, you didn't. I got 'im!" exclaimed the other. They could hear the thumping of an arrow on the ground as some impaled critter tried to get away. Both fellows rushed into the dark to get the coup de gras. Then the best shot of the night occurred. A howl of fowl oaths issued forth, as a shafted skunk shot two inebriated nimrods with his dying spray.

Even today, nearly 30 years later, when I drive down that mountain road, I can't help but smile.

The moral: Those drunk as skunks shouldn't sling shafts, because something shamefully stinky is sure to strike.

Horse Bow

The night wind was howling outside, and a winter rain pounded against my windows. A warm crackling fire danced in the fireplace, and I was cozying up next to it with a cup of chocolate and a good book. Barbara came into the room and asked, "Do you think we ought to have a garden this year?" She loves gardens when I'm the gardener.

"No, not this year." I apathetically replied with a twinge in my back.

"Okay," she conceded. She remembered my earlier trials at gardening and didn't push it anymore.

It happened almost 20 years ago, right after we moved to the country. This city boy decided to become a gardener. I started early one spring tilling and fertilizing the soil and carefully laying out the garden plots. With great care and exceeding work, it finally was planted by late spring. Things were going wonderfully well by mid-summer, then big problems occurred.

Three people lived across the road. They weren't much more than squatters. They lived in an old, run-down, single-wide trailer and made a subsistence on scams and cons. They also had a few head of horses for their own pleasure. They were likable enough people, but they had one big failing as far as I was concerned; they didn't feed their horses very well. Late every night, they would turn the horses out of their corral and let them graze in the neighborhood. Well, these horses soon found my garden to be Eden.

I complained to their owners, but they had the audacity to say that their horses were kept locked behind fences. No matter how much or hard I protested, they were always in complete denial. One day, I took a shovel-full of fresh manure that their horses had so kindly donated the night before and presented it to my neighbors as irrefutable physical evidence. "It must be from some other horses," they said. "Ours were locked up all night."

I was frustrated. Something had to be done. They were ruining my garden! An archer friend stopped by, and we went out and shot some aerial targets with flu-flus. Like falling bricks, it hit me. Why not use flu-flus on my equine friends? So, I proceeded to wrap cloth electrical tape around the rubber blunt points to a diameter of about two inches. Next, I took a light, 35-pound recurve and tried the flu-flus out. They seemed to be perfect. They hit with authority yet would not maim a horse. I was ready.

Late that night, I spied my quarry out among the carrots, two Boone and Crockett class horses that looked remarkably like my neighbors'. With the stealth of an Indian scout, I slipped around the back of the house and across the lawn to the garden. I quickly raised my bow and shot a flu-flu against the ribs of one marauding horse. It bounced off, and he let out a grand grunt and leaped away. The other departing horse was greeted by a well placed shot on his rump. I tore after them as they raced up the road. Chuckling, I saw them clomping along the blacktop, their steel shod shoes creating a fireworks of sparks, and their high whinnies permeating the night air.

"What's going on out there?" A nervous voice came from the neighbors' door.

"Oh, I just chased a couple of horses out of my garden. No need to worry...yours are always locked in their corral."

"What did you do to them? You didn't hurt them!" came the frantic voice.

"Don't worry," I replied. "I'm sure these horses are quite all right, just a bit excited... probably they're out by the highway now. Say, those weren't your horses were they?" As I happily walked back to the house, I could see the neighbors jumping into their old truck to chase after the long-departed nags. They didn't find them until the following day.

The neighbors kept a tighter rein on their horses the rest of that summer. My garden flourished, and we had a bountiful harvest. I even shared it with my neighbors. But old Fred seldom comes out a winner when he tries to deal out retribution. The neighbors kindly let me have all the horse manure I wanted for the garden that following winter, and I tilled it into the soil to

49

winter over. By spring, I had really rich soil to start anew. But I soon discovered that everything those horses ate showed up as seed in their manure, and my garden grew a sample of every noxious weed in the county!

When my wife mentions gardening, my back remembers the time it spent bent over pulling weeds, and it starts twitching and aching.

The moral: When you're horsing around and dealing out retribution, it may, in return, be dealt to you in unforeseen ways.

Ken Wilhelm pin-fletching arrows in 1945.

Chapter 5

STRAIGHT ARROWS

You can't imagine how excited I was when I went into the sporting goods store to buy my first broadhead arrow. Up until that time, I had been using cheap, 25-cent arrows. Now I was actually going to buy a real broadhead! I had carefully considered my purchase and knew that it would be worth the expense. This sporting goods store was a downtown store. It had carpeting throughout, and the walls were a taxidermist's delight with big game heads, fish, and birds everywhere. The store clerks wore suits and had very formal manners. I walked over to the archery department and gazed at the arrow selection. There I spied what I wanted: a white, cedar shafted arrow fletched with long, greybar feathers. It was tipped with a skeleton ferrule broadhead—all made by Ben Pearson. A clerk asked if he could help me. I pointed to the arrow and asked how much it cost. "One dollar and twenty-five cents apiece," he answered. A fortune, being that I earned about fifty cents a week on my allowance. But I stiffened to the trial and bought one.

A bit later in my training, I decided it was time to buy a dozen, matched, wooden target arrows. I went over to Frank Eicholtz's archery shop, and he sold me a dozen of Hugh Rich's best cedar arrows. They cost a treasure of $10.50 plus tax. I shot them at a target range in the park all that summer and literally wore them out. Back in those days, Hugh had a slogan of "straight as a Hugh Rich arrow." Even today, as I look over an exceptionally straight arrow, I will say, "This one's straight as a Hugh Rich arrow!" I got well acquainted with Hugh in his later years and told him about all this. He was really pleased. The feeling was mutual, because he told me that the bow I made for him was the finest he ever saw.

I bet that since man first started shooting arrows there has been a debate raging as to what constituted a good missile. It still rages to this day! But it has been said by many accomplished shooters that proper arrows are a bigger key to shooting success than a proper bow.

Indulge me, and let me give some concepts. There are countless shafting materials. Which one an archer chooses to use is his choice. In my opinion, there's no such thing as traditional and non-traditional shafting. My reason being that all of the materials function in the classical way—so it becomes a functional classification rather than a materials classification. Personally, I prefer wooden arrows, but nevertheless, I find nothing wrong with metal or plastics.

One of the big arrow challenges is finding a properly weighted shaft to efficiently accomplish the task. Arrows weighted for target shooting are better on the light side, whereas arrows weighted for big-game hunting should be heavier. Heavy arrows penetrate better than light arrows, but penetration is not a factor in killing a paper or foam target. A real hunting bowman has to sit down and make some intelligent choices concerning arrow weight in relation to the game animal being hunted. With deer-like animals, penetration is not too difficult with most any weight shaft. This is not so with the elk. It is a bigger and hairier animal, and heavy shafts are advisable. When a bowman decides to try to plug a wild boar, he really needs a strong, heavy shaft that will store enough energy to break open the frontal section of the pig and get to its vitals. If one underestimates here, the results could have deadly consequences for the shooter.

Composite and self-wood longbows handle heavy arrows very well. It is hard to overload their limbs with heavy shafts. If you own such a bow, it is foolish to use light-shafted arrows. Some long-handled, short-limbed recurves really get loaded down with heavy shafts. They do better with light shafts and maybe are not the most advisable bow for hunting large game where heavy arrows are more efficient. I am really happy to see the resurgence of the longer limbed recurve bows in the marketplace. They tend to be more stable and handle the heavier shafts better.

Fletching for the traditional arrow is almost always made from turkey feathers. Occasionally one will see goose, peacock, or some other feathers, but they are quite rare. The problem with turkey feathers is that they generally come from birds that are being raised for food. The feather itself is wasted protein. Researchers, over the years, have bred the bird with smaller and poorer quality feathers. Now, they even have a commercial turkey without any feathers at all! This may be great for the farmer, but it's bad for the archer. Back in "the good old days," there were large, strong, and oily greybarred feathers available cheaply. They made superior fletching. It was easy to get two 5 1/2-inch fletches from one feather. The white feathers were of better quality, too, but they were rarer and cost a lot more. It is the opposite today. The white feather is common, and the greybar is rarer and more expensive.

The very best fletching now is from the wild turkey. They are strong and naturally oiled for moisture protection. But, as you can imagine, they are very hard to procure. Many of my friends find farmers who raise greybar turkeys locally, and they make arrangements to get the feathers at slaughter time. A finer grade of fletching comes from their extra work. The greybar is stiffer and oilier than the white feather. This is an advantage to the hunter who shoots under moist conditions.

A number of us prefer a white or dyed white fletch. Our reasons being that it is easier to follow them visually. I had an episode with a big buck blacktail that brought this home. One dark and dreary afternoon, I was making my way across a hilly ravine. I spied this nice buck browsing in front of a hillside. He hadn't spotted me. I drew a quick bead on him with my greybar fletched-arrow and let it go. I immediately lost sight of the shaft because of the background and dismal day. The deer didn't even flinch but continued to eat. I couldn't tell if I overshot or undershot! I must have undershot, I thought, because I'd been doing that lately. I drew on him again and aimed a little higher. I released the arrow with the same results. I took another arrow from my quiver and aimed a little higher. I shot and lost sight again. Yet, there he stood, unaware. I grabbed another arrow, and with great determination I aimed higher still. I missed the deer, but he spotted me and bolted away. I went over to the scene of my mischief and discovered that all of my arrows had gone over him and not under as I had thought. Had I been using a visible fletch, I might have had a different conclusion to my tale.

But wait! A few years later, I was within 50 yards of the same area. Again, I spied a deer on the hillside. I drew a bead on it with a white fletched arrow. I let it go and could see the arrow pass harmlessly under the chest. The deer stood frozen. I pulled another arrow and aimed a touch higher. That arrow cut the deer's heart.

Greybar fletch is great for strength and moisture resistance, the white or dyed white fletch is good for vision. It might be advisable to use a four-fletch arrow, half greybar and half white.

This brings me to a question I'm often asked, "Which is better, three-fletch or four-fletch?" The answer is simple: neither, they both have their good points. The four-fletch can settle down an unruly broadhead well, and it straightens an arrow quicker off the bow. This is especially good for tree-stand shooting. It matters not which side of the arrow is against the bow, therefore the fletching will hold up better. This is an advantage with practice and target arrows. The four-fletch can be a more cost-effective alternative over the three-fletch. It is relatively easy to get two fletches of 4 1/2 inches each out of a single feather, whereas one can usually get only one 5 1/2-inch fletch. So, an arrow using four 4 1/2-inch fletches uses just two full length feathers, but three full length feathers are needed for a 5 1/2-inch, three-fletch arrow. The three-fletch arrow is quicker to make than a four-fletch. Because there is less wind drag, it is often quicker in cast also. I have had the privilege to shoot with some of the greatest field/target archers for over 40 years. From my conversations and observations with them, I conclude that excellent accuracy can be attained with either fletch style.

Three basic feather shapes are used: the parabolic; the shield; and what I call the primitive. I use all three with variations of each. From my study and observations, the parabolic shape is stronger (especially when moist), quieter, and quicker.

Probably the least attended chore of arrow-making is correct nock placement. Nocks that have been applied crooked, or out of alignment will cause inaccurate shooting. A wise arrow-maker is careful with this procedure. The type of nock used is basically a preferential choice by the archer. I like a style called a "Mercury Nock," (developed by Seattle Archery many years ago), because of its deep throat.

As previously related, all of the shaft materials perform the classical function. Aluminum has a wide spectrum of spines (please don't say splines) and weights, and it is readily available. Aluminum recovers very fast from the archer's paradox. It is great shaft material—especially for a recurve. It often gives a metallic ring when being shot, which can be bad for hunting. The aluminum-arrow industry spends hundreds of thousands of dollars each year propagating their material. The competition is very fierce for the archer's dollar. May I suggest that you follow their advertisements and enjoy all the high-tech hype that is put forth to entice you to use their products. It makes good reading.

There is a seemingly endless list of woods to use as shafting if one is inclined to make his own shafts. Also, one can find a variety of woods on the commercial market. Of course, the main type of wood shafting comes from the Port Orford cedar found in the Pacific Northwest. Oddly this tree is found naturally in Japan, too. Some speculate that ancient Japanese sailors brought seeds to the Northwest. As with any wood, Port Orford cedar varies from one tree to another, but overall it is fairly consistent. It is a straight-grained wood that splits easily and dowels well. Cedar doesn't warp readily and is moderately strong. In the 40's, 50's, and 60's, it was fairly plentiful. The major shaft-makers would go into the forests and find great "fall-down" logs. They would haul the logs out and split and dowel them. Good cedar shafting was cheap and plentiful then. I can remember getting all the shafts I needed in spines of 70 to 80 pounds and only 11/32" in diameter! By the 1970's, aluminum and glass shafting were in vogue. Several of the smaller wood-shaft manufacturers went out of business. The early 1980's found a resurgence in wood-arrow popularity. The remaining manufacturers were pushed to put out more stock. One leading shaft maker burned down and had to rebuild. The high demand and the lower supply had caused the price of cedar to rise. Then came the Japanese buying up cedar logs, and the federal government with new logging restrictions in old growth forests, and the cedar industry was almost shut down.

Just like with the bow-maker, the arrow-makers are looking for the perfect wood. Some woods make excellent shafts but don't lend themselves to high volume doweling. Some wood, like Douglas fir, makes excellent arrows, but the wood varies so much in physical characteristics that it is not suited to high volume manufacture. The very finest wooden shafts I have ever used were manufactured in Oregon many years ago by Bill Sweetland. They were compressed cedar called "Forgewoods."

Wooden shafting works really well with the self-wood bows. The reason is that wood snakes around a bow's arrow plate nicely, allowing for a good archer's paradox. Many, traditionalists make their own shafts and arrows to get the most exquisitely matched equipment.

I have had archers tell me that wooden arrows are not as accurate as aluminum. This is not necessarily true. I have witnessed that when cedar shafts have been highly matched in spine and weight and then shot in a shooting machine, their accuracy was the same as aluminum. The problem with woods is that they can warp and let down in spine. If an archer is careful, he can maintain a good set of wooden arrows a long time.

Back in 1965 I knew a state champion field archer. Our shop at the time had thousands of cedar shafts. He came over one night and selected a dozen shafts and matched them as close as I've ever seen. The following week, he made a beautiful set of arrows from them and then went to a state field tournament. When some of the other competitors (who used aluminum arrows) saw that he was using woods, they thought he had lost his mind. They didn't think that long, because he ended up winning the tournament. It was quite a coup. Yes, wood arrows are accurate.

This tournament spawned a big joke, also. We had this fellow who worked at our shop, that always gave us a hard time. He made himself a new set of aluminum arrows for the tournament. He left them in the shop the day before the shoot and went out on a chore. Some of the other boys at the shop pulled the points from his arrows, put a very small drop of mercury in each shaft, and then replaced the points. This poor fellow went to the tournament and, needless to say, his arrows did some strange things. He knew something was wrong but couldn't put his finger on it. We had intended to let him know of our mischief, but he was so stirred up that we feared telling him.

One of the most often asked questions when I make someone a bow is "What spine wooden arrows do I need with my new bow?" This is hard to answer because each person grips the bow differently, and releases the string differently. One bow may bend an arrow upon release more or less than another bow. I have made up a chart. It is just a general guide, but it can be used to give the archer a clue where to begin.

ACTUAL DRAW LENGTH

Bow Weight	25"	26"	27"	28"	29"	30"
45#	35-40	40-45	45-50	50-55	55-60	60-65
50#	40-45	45-50	50-55	55-60	60-65	65-70
55#	45-50	50-55	55-60	60-65	65-70	70-75
60#	50-55	55-60	60-65	65-70	70-75	75-80
65#	55-60	60-65	65-70	70-75	75-80	80 +
70#	60-65	65-70	70-75	75-80	80 +	80 ++
75#	65-70	70-75	75-80	80 +	80 ++	80 ++
80#	70-75	75-80	80 +	80 +	80 ++	80 ++

This chart is an average approximation of spines for arrows cut one inch longer than actual draw with a 125 to 150 grain broadhead. Some considerations: more centershot = less spine; heavier points = more spine; also feather length, release, and taper of shaft affects spine.

Another question people ask is "Are tapered shafts better than parallel shafts?" From my experience, I find that tapered shafts recover quicker from the archer's paradox. Well matched parallel shafts are just as accurate. When one needs all the weight possible in an arrow, the parallel shaft is the way to go. If one wants a quick recovering arrow that is not too sensitive, then go for the tapered shaft.

Arrows, like bows, are made for various purposes. There is one class of arrow I'd like to discuss. I call them rabbit arrows, stump-shoot'n arrows, or roving arrows. These are the arrows that I don't worry about losing or breaking. Every worthy bowman ought to have lots and use them.

I usually make mine in the hundred lot. I buy bulk spined shafts. They are dipped a couple of times in cheap lacquer and are not crested. I use full hunting length fletches, usually from feathers I've procured cheaply. I use blunts, "Judos," or field heads for points. These arrows shoot well and allow me the freedom to take outlandish shots that costly arrows inhibit. Most of the fellows that I go stump shooting with are insane. They take shots that nobody in their right mind would take. Of course, if I'd refuse to shoot at a target they'd picked out, I'd be marked as a sissy, lily-livered coward. Well, my inexpensive roving arrows really come in handy at times like these.

There is a magical charm to sit in one's den on a blustery winter's night and fletch arrows. With fletching jigs, feather burner, cresting lathe, and a small assortment of accouterments, one quickly falls into a therapeutic spell that can last for hours (or until the wife gets a whiff of a burning turkey feather). It is with hardy encouragement that I recommend this activity.

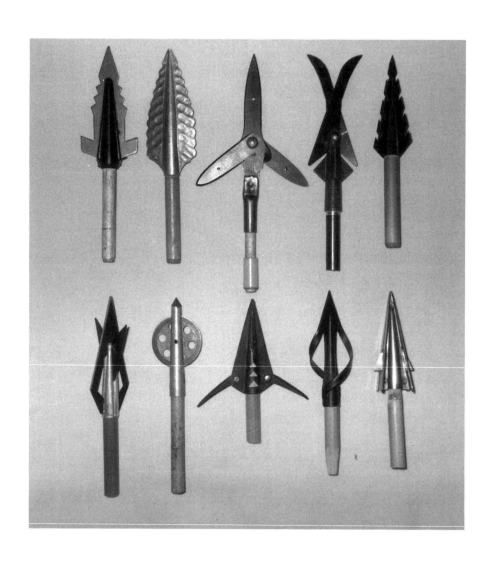

Chapter 6

THE CUTTING EDGE

I believe the most perplexing thing to the traditional hunting archer is what broadhead should be used. The array of commercial broadheads on the market today is mind boggling. The quality runs the gamut from crummy to fantastic. Likewise, the price goes from cheap to very expensive. Also, it seems that there is no shortage of broadhead "experts" to add to the confusion.

One fine summer day, a number of us archers were gathered under a ponderosa pine. Everyone present had numerous years of hunting experience. A curious thing often happens at these sorts of assemblies. The conversation deteriorates down to talking about broadheads. Being that everyone of us was an "expert" on the subject, we really got down to the nitty-gritty. It appeared that everybody had a different opinion as to what constituted a good broadhead, yet each archer was a successful hunter in his own right.

I've been a student of the broadhead since I bought my first one (a Ben Pearson skeleton ferrule) in 1952. I've listened, read, collected, and studied them with great enjoyment. I believe I've come up with one set of broadhead criteria to which most archers will subscribe. So I submit that this list be a guide:

1. Capable of being sharpened and keeping a sharp edge

2. Not excessively heavy

3. Of adequate width for the game being hunted

4. Not prone to windplaning

5. Structurally strong

6. Penetrates well

The main problem in studying the effectiveness of broadheads is that it is impossible to set up a true experimental design research. One cannot put arrow shooting machinery in a laboratory and shoot arrows into various animals from randomly selected positions and then check penetration and blood letting and the length of time it takes the animal to die. There have been some studies done on dead animals, but it is hard to draw any accurate conclusions. Most new archers give ear to shop owners and successful hunters about broadhead effectiveness. Articles on broadheads often appear in magazines that give advice. But, I believe that if an archer is seriously searching for a good head, he should consider my list of six criteria. Let's consider each, individually.

Capable of being sharpened and keeping a sharp edge

Some heads on the market cannot be sharpened. They have replaceable blades. Replaceable-blade heads have been around for a long time. Back in the early 1970's, a friend of mine, the late Duke Savora, started making a replaceable-blade head. It became very popular. I was pleased when he killed a grizzly with his new head using one of my bows. We had many conversations about broadheads. One thing he told me I was in complete agreement with. He said, "Fred, one of the main reasons I've developed my head with pre-sharpened blades is because there are great numbers of novice bowhunters that don't know how or won't take the time to sharpen their heads properly." There are numerous bowhunters who only pick up their bows for a few weeks of hunting season. They spend little time on equipment, and I guess the pre-sharpened heads are practical for them. From my own observations, the pre-sharpened broadhead styles do not penetrate very well.

I have always preferred to sharpen my own heads. Some are difficult because of ferrule circumference or multiple blade design. Occasionally a broadhead might be made with very hard steel (over 55 Rockwell), and this can be difficult. Soft steel is easy to sharpen, but it dulls too fast. Generally, a 45 - 55 Rockwell rating will be a good balance between sharpening ability and hardness.

Not excessively heavy

The weight of a head can be critical to good arrow performance. Heavy pointed arrows can play real havoc with the spine of an arrow. This is especially true with longer arrows. Shorter arrows are thrown out of balance easier with heavy points. I have friends who hunt exclusively from tree stands. Their longest shots are no more than 25 yards. They prefer big, heavy broadheads on heavy arrows that penetrate well. I understand and agree with their logic. On the other hand, the western archers who hunt in more open areas often take longer shots. They need flatter flying arrows with lighter points. All things being equal, however, it is usually wise to select the lighter head.

Of adequate width for the game being hunted

Time and time again, I've witnessed big game brought down quickly and efficiently with broadheads 1 1/4 inches wide or less. I also have witnessed considerable trouble with heads that are too wide or with too many blades. Broadhead blades also can act as steering vains on arrows. This always means trouble.

Not prone to windplaning

Windplaning broadheads are a real curse. Many years ago, I was hunting with a popular two-blade head that had an auxiliary bleeder insert. One afternoon, I settled myself in an old, abandoned apple orchard. I didn't wait long. A nice blacktail buck trotted into the orchard looking for downed apples. At eight yards away, it made a nice target—meat in the pot. I drew my arrow and focused on the chest. This animal was so close, I couldn't miss. I released, and to my surprise, the arrow ended sticking 15 feet up in an apple tree. I've never seen an arrow windplane as badly before or since. I theorized that the bleeder blade must not have been seated correctly, because I took the blade out and shot the arrow into a bank, and it went perfectly true. Auxiliary, replaceable bleeder blades are not structurally strong, either.

Structurally strong

Broadheads that bend or don't hold together well are to be avoided. Recently, I had a booth at a large traditional archery event. My friend, Ron Hoiland, had a booth next to me and was demonstrating the strength of his fine broadheads. His heads are works of art, and he uses exotic, true heat tempered steel. You just can't put a bend in them. He was demonstrating this by pushing the point down from its side onto a board. He would ask various fellows for one of their arrows for comparison, and then he would press the broadhead against the board and bend the tip. Ron would grin and say, "See, you have soft, untempered steel in your heads. I bet you didn't know that." This same scenario played on and on throughout the day. That evening, while we were eating supper, Ron mentioned that a number of archers were unaware that their broadheads were made from soft, untempered steel.

"Ron," I said, "I bet you're unaware that there are a number of fellows around here with bent points on their broadheads that would like to scalp you. You've ruined dozens of points today!" He then realized what he had done and we had a great laugh.

Back in the early 1960's, plastic ferruled broadheads became popular. During this time, I was hunting one bitter cold day in the rugged south-central Cascade Mountains of Washington. Hunters had sighted many deer that day. Several hunters had deer hanging in their camps. Right after dark, I was parked off the side of a forest road cooking chili on the tailgate of my Falcon wagon. Then I saw him. In the glimmer of my camplight, this fellow came stumbling up to my car. He was soaking wet and shaking all over. The temperature had to be hovering around zero, and I recognized that this guy was in a bad fix. It seems that he had gotten lost and fell into the river just before he found me. I put him in the warm car, gave him a steamy cup of chili, and drove him a mile over to his camp.

As he warmed up, he told me his sad tale. He had several shots that day at fine bucks. He even hit a few. But the arrows, upon striking, would bounce off the deer. It seems that the cold temperature made the plastic ferrules of his broadheads brittle and break upon impact. He was following one of the wounded deer that evening when he fell into the river. Luckily, he spotted my camplight and found me when he did. I wonder how many animals have needlessly suffered because of poorly constructed heads.

Penetrates well

I have seen enough game downed with arrows to know that deep penetration is a key to quick, humane death. Several factors inhibit penetration. Short wide blades and multiple blades are two factors. Thick fur and hides and bones are others. Howard Hill's advice that broadheads be about three times longer in length than in width is good for maximum penetration. Many of the finest hunters I know subscribe to this.

I have had a number of arrows actually stick into or penetrate bones. To eliminate this I slightly round the points of my broadheads so that my arrow will slide around the bone rather than stick into it.

Whenever you come across a true hard-core traditional hunting archer you will find a person who takes the study of broadhead points very seriously. Rightly so! After all, the hunting point is what accomplishes the task—that is our ultimate objective. Fortunately, today there are a number of fine broadheads on the commercial market. Unfortunately you will find more than a few "clinkers." Personal broadhead research is a very pleasant activity. Probably the only real drawback is that it makes the bowman an "expert;" subject to pontification at any gathering when some fool says, "What's the best broadhead?"

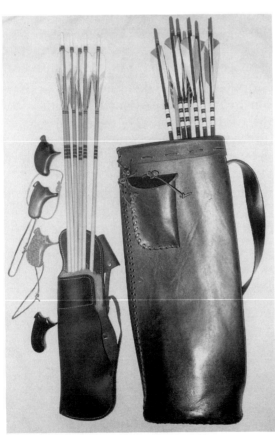

Four Eicholtz 'bowlocks,' Idaho 'Ranger' side quiver, and 'Hill style' back quiver.

Chapter 7

STORIES THAT LEAVE YOU ALL AQUIVER

Finding a good quiver has always been a challenge. It is easy to carry arrows, but to retrieve one arrow from the package can be a chore. To do this in a comfortable way is another problem. To have the arrows remain sharp is something else. One must add in that the arrows are to stay dry. Don't forget that the arrows must not rattle while being carried. The list of requisites goes on and on. Many novel ways have been invented to carry arrows. But there is no single best way. Therefore, it makes sense to use the type of quiver that best suits your purpose for the occasion.

I've been involved with quivers since I first started shooting. I remember my first good one. It was a small, leather, back quiver. If you use a quiver a lot, you'll gain a personal attachment to it. I literally wore that quiver out. Since then, I believe I've tried just about every kind of quiver: ground quivers, hip quivers, belt quivers, back quivers, pocket quivers, bow quivers, arm quivers, hand quivers, quivers of leather, quivers of skin, quivers of wood, quivers of canvas, and quivers of plastic and metal. You name it. I've tried it. I am still trying new quivers—that's the joy of it! One never gets tired of trying new ones.

One of my acquaintances is really partial to quivers. He has several dozen. Every time he goes to an archery event where someone is selling a quality quiver, he buys it. His problem is trying to decide which one of the multitude to use. People who buy and make lots of quivers need understanding spouses. One needn't have lots of quivers, however. A few well chosen ones will do fine. I'd like to offer some thoughts from what I've gleaned.

When an archer has to carry lots of arrows, back quivers are the best. There are many styles of back quivers, each with its own advantages and disadvantages. Small-game hunting and some target-shooting activities are well suited for back quivers. Back in the 1950's, on the field range, we packed at least a dozen arrows around. Large, leather, two strap back quivers with several compartments were the rage then. These quivers sat more upright on a person's back. I still use mine a lot at various 3-D shoots.

I find that the style of back quiver called a "Cat Quiver" or "St. Charles" quiver is very useful in rainy weather. The feathers are protected by a hood. When the "Cat Quiver" came out on the market a number of years ago, I was one of the first to use it. One wears this model directly down the center of the back. The top of the quiver reaches the back of the head and the bottom goes down to a person's butt. Two small, thin straps go over the shoulders. From the front, they look like suspenders. I took this quiver to the rain forests of the western Olympic Mountains elk hunting. It was ideal for the damp conditions. One afternoon, I was walking down a logging road heading for my car. I spotted a truck parked up ahead. There were a couple of fellows beside it who were also elk hunting. I walked up and stopped to say hello. We talked for a few minutes about our hunting. As I was about to depart down the road, one of the hunters surprised me by asking, "Say, don't you use arrows while hunting?"

"What do you mean?" I asked puzzled.

"I can see your bow, but where are your arrows?" he replied. I couldn't understand what he meant. I had a whole quiver full of them on my back. Then it dawned on me. From his perspective, as I walked up and talked to him, facing him the whole time, he couldn't see my quiver directly down the center of my back! I laughed and turned around. Then they both laughed as they saw the "Cat Quiver." They'd never seen anything like it before. Both felt a lot better. They thought that they had run into some kind of a nut who hunts with a bow and no arrows. (Now, wouldn't that be a real challenge?)

One of the best quivers for hunting is the type of back quiver Howard Hill preferred. An expression he used was, "My mother didn't raise any fools." When it comes to quivers, you can see he certainly wasn't a fool. Hill hunted all of his life and all over the world. A functional quiver had to be a must. From my experience, there are very few Hill-style quivers for sell that amount to much. The best ones are home or custom-made. Believe me, there are several critical concepts that need to be applied in the construction of this simple quiver.

A well made Hill-style quiver will carry a dozen or more arrows comfortably and quietly. It will easily slip from the shoulder or around the shoulder for easy passage through brush. It will present arrows effortlessly and quickly for rapid shooting. It will be easily adjustable in the strap for clothing. The leather will be heavy enough to hold the quiver's shape, but it will be flexible enough to collapse around the arrows.

There are times when back quivers are disadvantageous. They are no good if you have to carry a back pack on your hunt. (This happens a lot in mountain hunting.) It is tough to use them in tree stands. And the back quiver can be uncomfortable on a hot day.

One of my favorite arrow holders is the hip quiver. I like it for both target shooting and hunting. I have a nice, small, leather, target quiver that clips to my belt. It holds up to 8 arrows. It has a large zippered pouch and a pencil holder. I bought it from the great shooter, Jerry Amster, over 30 years ago.

I have never cared for the long tube-like belt quivers that are popular with some. They are fine on a lawn target range but not much else. Pope and Young used them in hunting and seemed to like them. They shake, rattle, and roll while you're moving and are always in the way.

For many decades, "Idaho Leather," out of Boise, has made a leather hip quiver called the "Ranger." It is about as slick a quiver as I've ever run across. This very adjustable, high quality quiver rides on the right-handed shooter's right hip. It incorporates a spring clip that holds up to six hunting arrows securely and quietly. Arrows come out of it smoothly and quickly with little motion or commotion. It swivels when going through brush and allows the use of a day pack while hunting. I know of two deer I've bagged because this quiver allowed me to quickly and quietly retrieve an arrow and nock it. A disadvantage is that it can only handle up to six arrows.

71

A very popular quiver is the bow quiver, but I don't know why. I have some and have used them, but I don't care for them. For one reason, it throws the bow out of balance and makes it twist in the hands while being carried. Another reason is that it makes the bow heavier. A bow quiver acts like a flag when one raises the bow to shoot at game. It often rattles when the bow is being shot. And rapid arrow retrieval is difficult.

On the positive side, a bow quiver puts everything in one place as a single unit. This is great if you are a road hunter or a poacher. Then you can just jump out of the vehicle and grab everything in one package. (Road hunters and poachers are not my idea of real hunters.) Archers on horseback like them, too. A bow quiver does keep your broadheads separated. And it does enable the archer to look over his arrow selection easily.

If an archer chooses to use a bow quiver for hunting, he should use it at all times because the bow feels different when it's on. He should also choose one that keeps the broadheads well protected; one should be very careful with sharp broadhead arrows.

I'm reminded of an accident which happened to a friend when we were on a winter deer and elk hunt in the mountains near Yakima. Six of us set up our camp at the base of the mountain. We had a large wall tent complete with a cookstove. This made camping more comfortable in the snow. In the mornings, we would drive up higher into the mountains and park and hunt from there. One morning, three of the fellows spotted several deer. They followed them into the brush. One fellow spied a nice buck 15 yards away. He took an arrow from his bow quiver as he stepped across a felled log. The arrow slipped from his hand, as it came from the quiver, and fell to the snow sticking point up. His leg came down upon the point driving it into his inner thigh. His broadhead was a real sharp two-blade with auxiliary bleeder blades. The head went all the way in up to the auxiliary blades. Luckily, the two other companions were there to apply first-aid and take him to Yakima to be sewn up. They got back to camp in the early afternoon. My friend was really very sore. The other two guys left him alone in camp and went back up the mountain hunting. My friend very soon became bored and restless. Shortly, a lady in a jeep stopped by the camp. She said she was looking for a hunting party on a certain logging road, but she couldn't find the road. My friend, tired of being in camp, consented to personally show her the road. But he warned her that he had a bad leg and couldn't walk, and she would have to drive him back.

He got into her jeep and noticed how terribly homely she appeared. He guided her up to the logging road, but the lady had amorous intentions. She took my friend way on down the road, all the while telling him how lonely she was. Finally, she stopped the jeep and suggested a little tomfoolery. My friend wanted no part of it. She warned him if he didn't oblige, she would leave him on that snow-laden mountain road. Consequently, he found himself standing on that lonely, mountain logging road unable to walk. Just after dark, some hunters in a truck found him and brought him into camp.

That night, as we sat in the warm tent eating our stew, my friend told of his day's adventures. When he got to the part about being cast upon the road, we all hooted. He looked at us and said, "Fellows, when you're a handsome hunk like me, you can't even go out into the wilds without some female trying to put her hooks on you." That really did stir up some glee!

I have seen enough archers to know that each individual will develop his own quiver preferences. My advice is for a person to be open-minded and try them all and never attempt to make one style do all things. Remember, there is a certain joy in acquiring quivers. Go ahead and treat yourself to a new one every now and then.

One of the experiences I really enjoy is going to a traditional archery gathering and observing the individualism displayed by various archers in their quivers. Modern commercial archery tends to make everyone look alike, from clothes to equipment. Traditional archery seems to celebrate the differences. Quivers used by the traditionalists testify to this.

Chapter 8

THAT STRING THING

Any of you old boys who have been arrow-flinging for a long time that say this is not true, don't know your bow-nock from your arrow-nock. Archery is a bloody, bruising sport! I know, because I've been bruised and bloodied ever since I first ran a fletching into the forefinger of my bow-hand when just a mere lad. A fellow just can't hang around bows and arrows without somehow losing a bit of hide.

In no way can I advise you on all the dangers of the sport, because there is an infinite variety. But I would like to advise you to be careful when asking an old-timer about his battle scars. You take my old friend, Bob, for instance. One time we were killing time in camp. I noticed that he had a pretty good cut on his thumb. Stupid me says, "How'd you get that cut on your thumb, Bob?"

"Well, let me tell you all about it. I was chipping arrow-heads the other night and ..." By the time he finished, I had been given a complete rundown of every personal bloodletting that archery had inflicted upon him. I have discovered that any bow-man, when given the chance, will readily pontificate about his owies.

With that out of the way, I'd like to tell you about a personal recurring owie. No, I'm not going to relate all the gore I've seen from upper bow-nocks whacking holes into peoples eyes and skulls as they unstring their bows, nor will I tell about irreverently used broadheads slicing off parts of the human anatomy. What I want to discuss is all the hurt I've sustained with that bow-string thing. The bow-string thing can bite a guy mainly in two places: the forearm and the string fingers. But there are other places it can grab you, too. Over the years I have been amply bitten. It seems that no matter how many precautions

I've taken, the bow-string thing always manages to get me—especially when I least expect it.

A dozen years ago, I foolishly rolled up my left shirt sleeve, put on my armguard, took my bow and arrows, and went to my range to do a little shooting. After a bit, that bow-string thing struck my sleeve-roll causing it to place a passionate kiss on my upper, inside forearm. I said, "Shucky darn." A couple of days later, I put on a short-sleeve shirt (I'm no fool), my armguard, took my bow and arrows, and went to my range to do a little shooting. After a bit, one of my arrow-nocks broke as I released it, and that caused the bow-string thing to interface with my upper, inside forearm once again. I distinctly remember saying, "Dirty, rotten, no-good shingly-fritz!!"

Shortly after that, a friend of mine sent me some flu-flu arrows. They were really nice. He had uniquely stapled the feathers to the shafts, along with gluing them for additional strength. I put on my short-sleeve shirt and marveled at the various shades of blue and purple that my entire inner arm displayed, from the hand to the elbow, as I put my armguard over the bruise. I grabbed my 70-pound bow and went out to do a little shooting.

My first shot would be for distance. I drew the flu-flu back as far as possible and turned it loose. There was a resounding crack at the moment of release (this was the shaft shattering in half where the staple held the feather). A most electrifying pain encompassed my whole left side as the bow-string thing bit into my bicep and down across my inner elbow until it went underneath my armguard, all the while eating my flesh on its quick, destructive, vibrant journey. Blood burbled up through the puffy, purple mounds that were my former bruises. Recovering my voice, I said in my best oration, "Oh my, that certainly does smart!"

Doc Kenagy, great northwest archer of the 40's and 50's.

Section II

SHOOTING

Hugh Rich's excellent form with a 75-lb. bow in 1948.

Chapter 9

HOW TO SHOOT THE DOGGONE THING

Do you remember the first time that you seriously tried to shoot a bow? Most of us couldn't even pull the arrow back without it falling off the shelf, let alone aim the thing. After a novice shooter begins to acquire an ability to handle the bow physically, he then has the frustrating task of learning how to aim. It's at this point that lots of contention and confusion come into the sport. It seems that there are two ways of aiming: bow-sighting devices, and instinctive shooting. I remember, as a young lad, that there were two classes of shooters, each subscribing to one method of aiming or the other. Each class was very vocal and prejudicial towards the other. I even witnessed a fist fight over this. Today, there are still vestiges of this contention.

It seems natural to aim with a sight any weapon we try to employ. Maybe this comes from our firearms inheritance. Real efforts to use aiming devices on bows didn't appear seriously until right after World War II when new synthetic materials were developed. These plastics helped to make the archery bow less breakage prone. Up to this time, most bows were made from wood. If a wooden bow is held at full draw for the time it takes to use a sight properly, it weakens the bow and hastens breakage. Because of this, a quick aiming and shooting style was employed.

After the war, people enjoyed more leisure time. This led to archers spending increased time with target and field archery. Higher scores became more important. This led to sight-shooting and more complex archery gear. The evolution has finally bloomed into a new sport. This new sport does not resemble traditional archery.

Sighting devices on bows are not accepted in the traditional archery fraternity. So, when an aspiring archer takes up the traditional mode, he can eliminate learning to use a sight. But, there are still some hard choices to be made; and there are grave consequences for those choices. Let me describe the options and consequences now.

When one discuses how to shoot a bow, he usually goes into proper form and how to aim. I have a different approach. I like to start by discussing the brain, and how it operates in relationship to shooting. Now, you've heard the tired old cliché of the simile that the brain is like a computer. This is a very good comparison, however. The brain is the great operations center for the body. When you introduce a new function, such as shooting, the brain has to assimilate all of the new information and then act upon it. The brain receives all new external information through the senses. So, when learning to shoot, it is important that correct information gets to the brain so it is not confused. The brain hates being confused, and therefore it works over the information until some concept is made, even if it is an incorrect one. Consequently, the task of the archer is to program the brain correctly into the integrated shooting process. We usually call this programming process "practice."

There are two parts of practice: (1) practice to perfect the physical aspects of pulling and releasing the arrow, and (2) practice to program the brain on the aiming process. It is very difficult for the brain to handle both types of practice at the same time. In fact, practicing to perfect your release at the same time as working on your aiming picture is a futile effort.

Learning to shoot is a thinking process. Carrying on internal conversations with ourselves improves thinking. Being aware of how the brain learns something like shooting a bow and arrow is called "metacognition."

Meta = about

Cognition = thinking

Metacognition = being aware of your own thinking/learning processes.

One-half to two-thirds of us engage in metacognition anyway, therefore, it is wise to use it more effectively to shoot better. Most real good shooters that I know, say things to themselves like this when shooting: "Turn the head more directly to the target. Turn the head more directly to the target." Saying this alerts the shooter to the fact that the brain gets a better visual picture of the target than when he is glancing at it out of the corners of his eyes.

Thinking is the manipulation of sensory data, especially kinesthetic (physical touching and feeling) and visual data, in the shooting process. Auditory data plays a role, too. Research shows that when an archer has an understanding of how he learns (how the brain handles sensory data), he will be a better shooter.

The brain has two sides, or hemispheres, the right and the left. Each hemisphere is responsible for certain learning operations. A lot of the shooting process is a right-hemisphere operation. Sometimes, when you want to more effectively instruct the right hemisphere, it is best to do it with music. Therefore, it might be advantageous for the shooter to sing to himself, "Turn the head more directly to the target." The right hemisphere is also turned on when a person brings his weight from the bottoms of his feet to the balls of his feet.

Learning to physically shoot a bow takes lots of time and study. Each of us is individually different. Consequently, each of us will have a slightly different form. If you go to a Major League baseball game and observe a team, you will notice that every one of the nine batters are excellent hitters. You will also notice that no two hitters approach the act of batting with the same exact form. Their batting form conforms to their own individuality. I know more than a few archers who try to copy the shooting form of Howard Hill to a tee. Heck, I've even tried to myself. The truth of the matter is that not all of us are very good when we do. We are different than Howard. I'm not saying that his style was wrong; he had super form. The principles that he ascribed to are correct. But there are other styles and principles, even if they be ever so slightly different, that may be better for your physical and mental make-up.

There are some constants to good shooting form. Consistency in drawing, anchoring, and releasing are most important. There are many theories written on how an arrow is to be drawn,

Three-time national champion, Erwin Pletcher, of the 1940's may be all-time best.

*Few people can outshoot British Columbia champion shooter, John Kellow,
and his 80-lb. longbow.*

anchored, and loosed. Let me tell you some thoughts from my point of view.

A bow should be drawn mainly with the back and shoulder muscles. When full draw is reached, the pressure will also be held in the back and shoulders. Most great shooters subscribe to this—even Howard Hill. New shooters, who want to conform to the quick draw and release (snap shooting) method, often fail to achieve the amount of draw necessary to transfer tension from the arms and shoulders into the back. Consequently, very poor habits are programmed into the brain.

The position of the archer's feet is an important consideration when it comes to reaching a proper draw. When one stands in the classic fashion of being at a right angle to the target, with an imaginary line drawn from the toes of one foot to the toes of the other foot and then to the target, it is physically easier to transfer the bow's power into the back muscles. If the right-handed shooter employs an open stance, with the right foot in front of the left, and the head and body facing the target more directly, it is a bit harder to get the right shoulder back far enough where the inline pressure is transferred from the right arm to the archer's back. Therefore, new shooters will often have more pressure in their right arms and fingers than necessary. This leads to the bad habit of plucking the string and throwing the right hand away from the face. When one continually does this, he is programming his brain with false information. I'm not saying that the open stance is bad, but as one learns it, he should be aware of the importance of getting the drawing arm and shoulder back far enough for the back muscles to hold the pressure.

Learning proper drawing form using lighter weight bows really helps the aspiring bowman.

With all the popularity in recent years of traditional archery, there are many so- called "experts" making videos and writing columns in magazines giving shooting advice. Some of these people are more adept at using words than using good shooting form. I think they expound to feed their egos or pocketbooks. The other night, I went to the video store to rent a movie for my wife and myself. On the rental shelf was a video about how to shoot the traditional bow. It starred some guy who has set himself up as an "expert." Well, I rented it out of curiosity, and what a laugh it turned out to be. This fellow could hardly hit a thing; but worse yet was his terrible plucking of the bowstring. Upon releasing the string, his hand would fly out from his face. He admitted to the problem. I think if he would have used a lighter bow, closed his stance a bit, and come to a complete power draw, with his back muscles supporting the draw, his plucking problems would have been lessened. His brain would need reprogramming, however.

Another aspect of drawing a bow has very important ramifications. The bow arm should push as the string arm pulls. This equalizes dynamic forces so that the muscles expand on both sides of the body instead of collapsing when the arrow is released. This concept is especially true when using heavy, hunting-weight bows. If a person holds his bow arm out straight and then proceeds to draw, he may have a tendency to collapse the bow arm (even if it is ever so slightly) upon release, he will get an arrow that goes to the right (for a right-hander) or left (for the lefty). The opposite is true for the archer who pushes too hard with the bow arm. The trick, then, is to apply equal push-pull pressure. One has to remember that this push-pull pressure has to be consistent throughout the complete shooting session. If not, his brain may start reacting to the inconsistency and form another bad habit. For years, I've watched people over-bow themselves. They might be able to shoot 20 to 30 arrows strongly and accurately, but they will go to a practice session or an archery gathering and exceed their limit. This is not an occasional occurrence but a regular happening. Good shooters choose the correct weight bow for the number of arrows they shoot.

As I earlier mentioned, there are two parts of practice. A wise archer it is that sets himself very close to the target butts and practices standing, drawing, anchoring, and releasing—doing it over and over again until his brain is receiving constant correct feedback. As this continues day in and day out, his physical motions are becoming automated. Actually, his brain is forming new learning paths called dendrites. When the brain has fully learned the shooting task, the archer will have that smooth,

Ed Kellow shows the form that wins championships and gets game.

consistent, exact form that is so coveted. But this all takes exacting work which is often times dull and repetitive. Some good shooters even close or cover their eyes during these sessions to more fully insure that physical form is all that the brain is programming.

When the brain can recognize correct physical form, it is then time to teach it how to aim. Think about it. Doesn't it make sense? The brain now can concentrate on how to get an arrow to the target without having to compensate and adjust for shooting form inconsistencies! Again the wise archer steps up close to the target and practices only on hitting the target. Being that he is so close, it is easy. This teaches the brain what is wanted. The brain needs to have several repetitions of hitting the target in order to develop automated learning. Next, the archer may practice at various distances.

Make no mistake about it, the brain does aim the arrow with information received from the senses, mainly visual clues. In order for the brain to have a positive visual bearing in aiming, a lot of us use the point of the arrow for a frame of reference. Some archers claim they do not use anything to aim with. They just concentrate on the target and let 'er rip.

In reality, the brain is using lots of visual clues and instantly relays commands to the muscles on where to hold and release. People who shoot without the point-of-arrow reference have a quicker aim and are very automated in their shooting. They also run the risk of having the brain easily confused. It is especially important to concentrate on the target so much that nothing but the target is viewed. "Tunnel vision aiming" it is sometimes called.

The arrow point reference is used by most "instinctive" archers to one degree or another. It is often called point-of-aim, split-vision, and gap-shooting. Those who concentrate on the arrow point are using "point-of-aim," and those who reference the distance between the arrow point and the target are "gapping" or "split-visioning."

When a person has a "loosey-goosey" form (i.e., inconsistent on drawing, anchoring, and releasing), he often forsakes

Tom Cole in a very relaxed position.

Perfect follow-through of five-time national champ, Erwin Ketzler.

Great contemporary Michigan archer, Ron LaClair.

Bob Wesley demonstrating proper in-line power draw.

the arrow point in aiming, because it really has no visual meaning to the brain. Therefore, this type of traditional shooter uses
what is sometimes referred to as pure instinctive shooting. This
allows the brain to freely search for the right aiming spot and
relay messages back to the body in a come-hell-or-high-water
way. The brain, the marvelous organ that it is, often times comes
through and does wondrous things for an archer. I use the loosey-
goosey form when shooting aerial targets and moving targets. I
seriously practice it. But, when it comes to shooting targets and
game, I use a gap arrow-point method that is more accurate on
stable targets.

The great archer, Bob Wesley, uses his power draw and arrow-point aim very effectively on all targets—moving and
stable—as did Howard Hill. Like so many good shooters I know,
Bob spends countless hours working on proper form and aim.
Good shooters get that way with good practice. There is no short-
cut to shooting success. It takes internal will power, time, com-
mitment, and a degree of intelligence. I have often thought that
a lot of duffers in golf would be better players if they paid more
attention to practice and less to playing a round of golf. Many
instinctive archers would have more success if they'd spend more
time on practice and less time going to weekend 3-D shoots.

I have a friend in California, Joe, who loves to shoot at long-
distance targets. He practices continually at ranges up to 200
yards with his heavy bows. Joe is very serious about his shooting form. He has to be, because at long ranges even the slightest
glitch in form would be disastrous. Joe understands the importance of drawing the arrow to the same exact anchor and having
proper tension in both arms, shoulders, and back. You can bet
that his release is crisp and smooth. I watched him put on a real
show in Pennsylvania last year on long-range targets at a big,
traditional shoot. A ground squirrel at 100 yards is in real danger when Joe's in the field!

Many shooters use the loosey-goosey style. Most of them
are hunters. Their form is not bad. It is just unorthodox. This
kind of shooter may stand with his feet in any number of positions—it makes no difference. He may cant his bow on one shot,
leave it vertical on the next, and have it horizontal on the next,

depending on the circumstances of the shot. He may draw 25, 26, or 29 inches. His anchor hand might float away from the face. To be good at loosey-goosey, certain things always happen: the release is clean and smooth; and the bow-arm is always steady.

This style is not too good for most who like to go to archery contests and get high scores. The amount of concentration needed is too much for the target game. It is, however, great for the hunter, who quite often is forced to make quick, accurate shots under the most demanding of circumstances. A friend of mine was hunting elk one crisp, cold morning. In front of him was a large, fallen log. He heard some elk crashing through the brush on the other side of the log. Instinctively he jumped up on the log for a better look. What he saw was the last cow elk heading smartly into the brush. Worse yet was that he was standing on a slick, icy covering of dew. Quickly and under acrobatic stress, he shot a perfect arrow into her ribs before his feet slid off the log.

I have seen loosey-goosey shooters ridiculed at archery events because of their form. This is not right. This style definitely has advantages in some circumstances. What is worse, however, is when a loosey-goosey shooter goes to an archery tournament and doesn't shoot up to par and then criticizes himself for poor shooting.

When I was a young man, in my late twenties, I had a very stodgy power form. It had served me well. I could (and did) shoot with the best of archers and not be shame-faced. Then, one weekend, I went to the Potholes area of central Washington state to try carp shooting. An experienced carp shooter had given me information on the right arrows, fish points, bow-reels, etc., and a place to find lots of carp. I had a little experience shooting sharks and rays in saltwater as a teenager, but this carp business was new to me.

Central Washington state is an agricultural marvel. Right after World War II the federal government started up a multi-billion dollar transformation project of damming the Columbia River and irrigating hundreds of thousands of acres of fertile, dry, desert lands into rich productive farmlands. Carp had some-how been introduced into the Columbia River system, and I was about to start into one of the most fun activities an archer can do. At the time, I didn't realize this.

The spot where I was guided, was an irrigation runoff creek that poured into a large, man-made, desert lake. In the late spring, carp by the thousands would migrate up the murky creek to spawn. The fisheries department appreciated anyone who would shoot the carp, because this fish would ruin game fish spawning beds.

I stepped up to the creek, as instructed, and peered into the chalky water. After a bit, I spied a carp swimming up the current. I had to be fast and wasn't. I couldn't come to my power-draw and aim quickly enough. I'd see a dark fish shape swimming under the milky current for an instant, and then it would disappear. After a couple of desperate hours, I was really frustrated. There was one place in the current where they frequently showed themselves briefly. I decided to focus on that spot, and when a dark shape appeared, I would make a quick, loose draw and shoot. Well, up came a fish, and I quickly let off a shot. I got it! Over time, I learned to quick-draw and release. It was the only way to get these carp. After several trips to this carp haven, I was making some outstanding shots with my loosey-goosey form.

It is amazing how well a person can shoot when he lets his well-practiced instincts take over the shooting process. Do you remember when you learned how to drive a car? The first few times shifting the gears and pushing the clutch, etc., was a real struggle. The more you did it, the easier it became. Now, when you drive to the store, you are not conscious of any shifting, braking, steering, or switch turning. It is all automatic for the brain and muscles. Have you ever watched a good basketball player as he weaves and dashes towards the basket? He suddenly jumps, shoots, and swish. He used no sighting device. He integrated well-practiced coordination, form, some experience, concentration, and an instinctive feel that the brain messaged throughout his body.

Those who employ a deliberate, power, instinctive form may be ridiculed, too, because of their seemingly slow shooting process. This is wrong. Deliberate shooting can be very effective, as witnessed by how good Howard Hill was with it. Hill had worked and practiced on his power form so much, that his shooting process seemed effortlessly smooth and quick. People who are new to archery are often under the misconception that his shooting style was loosely formed, and that he was a completely instinctive shooter. In reality, Hill had a very well-defined shooting and aiming style.

Whatever method of instinctive shooting an archer chooses, however, practice is the key; practice to develop coordinated muscles, practice to program the brain on how to aim, practice on concentration, practice, and more practice to make perfect. A wise hunter will also practice the process of quickly and efficiently nocking arrows. I am told that Art Young would spend whole sessions doing no more than taking arrows from the quiver and nocking them.

Part of your practice routine should be at moving targets. With regular practice, the traditional shooter can become very proficient on moving targets. On a previous hunt, I was stalking a large mule deer doe that was somewhere in front of me. As I stepped into a cleared area, she jumped from behind some sage going full speed for other parts. Instinctively, I pulled my arrow past the deer and shot it into her vitals. I've taken countless game which have been on the move, not because I'm a great shot, but because I'm familiar with this type of shooting.

My friend, and longtime archer, shop owner, and bowmaker, Cecil McConnell, is an expert on moving targets. I've watched him win many moving target events at archery gatherings including a running deer target at a large, western traditional longbow shoot. We were at one such shoot in the early 1980's. The event had many moving targets, which he was drilling. We came to this one target that was a large pole about eight feet tall. It was slowing turning at the base. On the pole was a huge python that twisted its way up to the top in a barber pole effect. The head of the python target had a bull's eye ring which was about two inches in diameter. With the pole turning, the python gave the appearance that it was snaking its way up. There were six of us in the shooting group, and we seemed to be having a difficult time with the optical illusion. I felt lucky to get one of my two arrows into the body at the 20-foot shooting distance. The last shooter was old Cecil. He raised his longbow as the python's head came into view, and shot his first arrow into the ring. "What a lucky shot!" we all chanted at him. (We do our best not to let anyone in our shooting party get a swollen head. It's for their own good, you understand.)

"Just to prove to you gentlemen that that first shot was no accident, I shall do it again," Cecil said wryly. And with that, he raised his bow and shot another arrow into the ring on the serpent's head. This, my friend, is one of the best shooting demonstrations I have ever witnessed. We all gathered around Cecil and pounded his back and reveled in his fine demonstration.

Cecil, along with countless other good archers, actively practices hitting moving targets. A good way to do this is to make a target that moves on a rope and pulley down an incline. Bob Wesley, on his Poplarville, Mississippi, range, has a wild boar target that comes out of the trees straight towards the archer. Practice on this target came in handy for him when he was charged by a real, live, red-eyed boar while hunting.

I especially enjoy getting with my shooting friends to practice shooting thrown disks on the ground or in the air. It is also fun to shoot at released helium-filled balloons. In some places, out in the West where the jackrabbit abounds, it can be tremendous practice and fun to shoot them on the move. When you get good at shooting bunnies, you may then aim at only their long ears. The Wilhelm brothers called this "ear-whacking." They even rigged up an unmanned old jalopy that would go in a large circle dragging a target behind on the flat desert.

When one is a serious archer, he pays especial attention to gripping the bow. There are many ways to grasp the bow, but I'd like to discuss just two. The archer that shoots real heavy bows needs a strong grip. This calls for using the whole palm of the hand as a solid perchment. Many who do this prefer a bow grip that is slightly concave or straight at the point where it rests across the palm. This enables the hand to more fully control the pressures that a heavy bow imparts. It is natural for the shooter to collapse his wrist while doing this. Some people call this healing the bow. In order to line up his sight picture, the archer will often bend his bow-arm elbow slightly.

Another way of gripping the bow is to put most of the pressure in the area at the base of the thumb. Archers who do this often prefer what is called a pistol or slight pistol grip. This style works better with bows that are lighter. It is a very accurate way to grasp a bow. The bow-hand wrist is not fully collapsed. The archer's elbow is not as bent as with the other style. In fact, it is usually straight.

I know people who effectively interchange both styles of gripping, depending on what bow weight is being employed. When an archer sets forth to purchase a fine new custom-made bow, he should have these things in mind. A novice archer should explore the grip styles and make some intelligent choices of how he wishes to grasp the bow.

Getting a new bow to shoot right (tuning a bow) can be very difficult—especially for a neophyte. Let me tell some procedures that I find effective.

The first thing I do is string the bow and check its brace height. The brace height is sometimes called a fistmele. This is an Old English unit of measure which defines the distance between the widest parts of a person's fist with the thumb fully extended. The thumb tip is placed on the bowstring, and the bottom of the fist should touch the handle of the bow. This doesn't work with all people, but it does for me, because I have a 6 5/8 inch fistmele. It seems that many centuries ago, English yeomen soldiers were apportioned a serving of food according to the size of their closed fist. Sometimes a soldier would be really hungry, therefore, he'd extend his thumb to make his fist appear larger—thus we get the term "fist meal" (fistmele).

Bows that are strung too low will be smoother, quicker, and very prone to cause the arrow to slap across its arrow plate upon release. This usually causes a side-to-side fishtailing motion of the arrow. Bows that are strung too high have a stacking draw, and they are somewhat more prone to damage. High strung

Notice "deep hook" finger placement by perhaps the best competitive archer who ever draw a bowstring, Rube Powell, five-time national champion of the 1950's.

bows generally don't kick as much upon release. So, ideally, the bow will be strung somewhere in between. On my hunting bows, I prefer the fistmele to be as low as possible and still get good arrow flight. On field and target bows, I do the same as with the hunting bows, but I increase the fistmele 1/4 to 1/2 inch higher. Because of variations in people's forms, there are no standard fistmele lengths.

Most archers shoot with a Mediterranean release—i.e., one finger over the arrow nock and two under. This causes unequal dynamic pressures on the bow's limbs. A three-finger-under release does this even more so. Bow-hand pressure adds into the mix. Therefore, if one nocks his arrow so that it would be a true 90 degree angle from the string, it would more than likely porpoise up and down upon release. To compensate for unequal dynamic tension, archers nock their arrows about 1/8 to 1/4 inch above 90 degrees on the string. I find it helpful to shoot at a target 50 to 60 yards distant when checking for nocking-point placement. This distance allows me to follow the shaft flight over a distance. If any wobbling occurs, I play around with the nocking point until the arrows fly correctly. Some people prefer the nocking point button below the arrow nock, and others prefer it above. Some even have a button above and below; this is very good for target shooters, but it can be inconvenient for hunters. I have personally found that some bows shoot better with the arrow over the nocking point, and others shoot better under it.

If my arrows are of proper spine, and shoot straight, but go to the right of the target, I sometimes build out my arrow plate (right-handed shooter). If they go to the left, I usually increase my arrow spine a bit.

Another tidbit of knowledge to think about is how bow length and bow design affect arrow tuning. Some recurve bows have very floppy, sensitive limbs, and it is difficult to keep all of the dynamic pressures in check in a consistent way. The slightest variation in shooting form causes all kinds of havoc. Short bow lengths do the same thing. As a bow gets shorter, the angle of the string increases on the string fingers, and arrow-flight consistency decreases.

This is why a number of us prefers longer bows. It is a common and amusing sight to see poor and mediocre shooters using moderate and short length bows, exhibiting poor results, because of the sensitivity of their equipment. (Watch out! Here I go to my pulpit. "Today's lesson is on the inherent evils of the short bow. There are many who would tempt you into buying that neat little bow—if you succumb, woe be unto you!! Amen.")

Chapter 10

A-ROVING

Let's go a-roving with our gang.
The fields and meadows do beckon.
Come out and let the bowstrings twang.
Across nature's vale we'll reckon.

What is the finest shot you've ever witnessed? I can recall many, but the absolute best has to be one a friend of mine made in 1967, while we were out stump shooting. I had built a recurve bow for a fellow who worked with me at Seattle Archery. I arranged to go with him to a wooded stump field one evening after work for some sport at roving. When we arrived at our destination, I presented the bow to my friend, Jack. He walked straight over to a canyon and nocked an arrow. "What are you going to shoot?" I asked, because I couldn't see a suitable stump in front of him.

"That cedar stump down the hill there, " he replied.

I was dumbfounded. That stump was well over two hundred yards down the hillside. Jack raised the bow and launched the maiden shot. I stood transfixed, as the arrow arched through the sky and down toward the stump. A muffled thud greeted us, as the arrow struck the center of the target! I was completely amazed. The first arrow shot from that bow could not have been cast any further; the target was at the extreme outer limits.

Many pleasant memories and amazing tales have been initiated by my trips afield, over the years, in pursuit of the wily stump.

Target archery was one of my major endeavors as a youth. In those days, many of us so-called target archers were very aloof. We believed that proper form and deportment were established by practice on the green lawns. A degrading label of "stump-shooter" was given to the hunting type of archer who did not participate on the target range but rather in stump fields. Eventually I changed, and I'm now a real, genuine-to-the-core, dog-eared stumpshooter, and proud of it. When field archery's founders were active in their sport during the beginning of this century, a major portion of their shooting was at stumps and other natural targets. These men were a hardy lot who enjoyed taking their equipment into the wilds. They discovered that their accuracy on game increased when they practiced in a stump field. These pioneers created a game they dubbed "roving." A group of hunting friends would pack up their archery gear and a little grub and head out to the wilds for a day or two. One bowman would select a target at random such as a stump, bush, or maybe a clay bank, and all would take a shot in turn. The archer with the closest arrow would get a point, a nickel, or whatever, and have the honor of choosing the next target. I can tell you that when I'm with my wild rover friends some of them really pick some tricky shots, but this is target shooting at its finest.

Stump shooting is good therapy for the hunter. Unlike field archery ranges, the archer is confronted with targets that simulate real hunting conditions. This definitely sharpens the eye and trains the mind to judge distance. The bowman never tires of the repetition of shooting at the same target; every stump can be a new and different target. One can get well acquainted with his hunting tackle, especially the bow, in the stump field. I know of at least two deer I've bagged where most of the credit has to go to a prior stump-hunting expedition. Stump shooting also gives the archer a chance to get the feel of the outdoors more often, and that's what really adds up. Personally, as a bowyer, stump shooting allows me a chance to make some field studies on my bows.

I recall an outing when some hunting friends and I planned a day in a beautiful, coniferous forest on the lower, western slopes of the Cascade Mountains. We packed our lunches, archery tackle, and fishing gear (fishing fever often strikes suddenly, and we need medicine in the form of a rod and reel to help overcome such attacks). After a little drive, we reached our secluded spot. This was the start of a happy day's shooting.

The competition on stumps really got keen. Often, one of us would be saying something like this; "See that black spot on that little stump over there? Well, you ain't got a hair on your chest if you don't hit it before I do." The rest of us, not wanting our egos hurt, would accept the challenge.

We generally try to select a certain spot on the stump to hit, not just the whole thing. The results are the same as shooting at game. If we draw on the whole target, we may easily miss, but if we concentrate on a small spot, chances are better for a good hit.

As the day wore on, we killed stump after stump. We even got in a little fishing, too. Of course, on the last few stumps, we had a wager of a hamburger and milkshake going.

Many times, while on these excursions, I have been rewarded with shooting at small game. Often, I've had shots at crows, foxes, squirrels, coyotes, rabbits, and other critters. The archer had best be acquainted with local game laws before shooting, however. One friend of mine was doing some stump shooting in a legal deer area, when he came across three deer. Having a few broadheads with him, he neatly bagged a nice doe.

Most all regions of the U.S. and Canada have logged off areas that are ideal for roving. Here, in the Pacific Northwest, we have an abundance of stumps left over from multitudes of logging operations—big old rotten cedar stumps, smaller fir stumps, what splendid targets they are! Some places do not have stump fields, however. Don't fear, while in Texas I substituted by shooting into clay banks of the arroyos. In some parts of California and the Southwest, I've used sagebrush as targets.

If you find that the winter doldrums have you aching to get out, or maybe you're weary of punching paper on a straw bale, or you might be a novice wanting to learn your weapons, or you could be an old dog looking for new tricks, then I give you a challenge to get out and bust some stumps. If you are already a stump killer who enjoys this facet of traditional archery hunting, you know its benefits.

Sylvan Archers of Oregon at a shoot in the 1940's.

Chapter 11
THE SHOOT

During the early era of mankind, various groups and clans of our ancestors would meet in archery contests to prove themselves. It has been suggested that some of these contests were sham battles that eliminated the need for open warfare. Toxophilite tournaments have carried down through the centuries, sometimes with scant popularity and sometimes in vogue. Today, in America, traditional archery contests and events are fairly common. These gatherings of modern-day archers are not conducted to decide warfare questions, more often than not, the scoring isn't even contested. What makes archery events popular now, is that they are fun.

Many people refuse to participate in these popular events, generally referred to as "shoots." They may feel intimidated by their lack of shooting prowess or their newness in the sport. This is a shame, because there are many novices and others with various abilities at these gatherings, and there are numerous things for one to enjoy.

Life-like, 3-D animal targets are placed in simulated hunting situations. Moving and aerial targets are often presented. While most people go for the shooting, traditional archery manufacturers, dealers, and vendors are usually there hawking their wares, which adds color and interest. A great deal of information can be gleaned from them. Often seminars and shooting demonstrations spice up the events. For me, the real fun of these shoots is seeing my old friends and meeting new ones.

Our culture is defective in the way we lack honor and respect for our elderly. I believe we inherited this from our participation in industrialized society—if a person is too old to have a job, then he is excess baggage. Most other cultures hold a special reverence for their elders. They understand the pool of experience and wisdom in this segment of the population. Maybe we ought to change some of our notions and glean from our seniors. One phenomenon that I have observed at archery events through the years is what I refer to as the "retired archer." As a young man, I recall seeing old men come to archery tournaments and just hang around and not do any shooting. It seemed that the trials of aging had reduced them to observers of the sport. They would seek out from among the participants, a willing, listening ear. I loved their stories and companionship. They still come to archery events, and I still love their stories; but now, as I grow into a more advanced age, I agonize with them in their infirmities. I met a gentleman at a Pennsylvania traditional archery shoot this last year. He was suffering from a bad shoulder, which he hoped would soon heal and allow him to shoot again, but we both knew it was hopeless. We conversed about his lifetime of archery for awhile, then his eyes started watering. The pleasure of being amongst archers, and the pain of knowing that he couldn't shoot was almost too much for the poor chap. A wise archer it is that seeks out these old patriarchs and gleans from their wisdom.

Most anyone that attends archery events will meet some real good shooters. Being in company with good shooters helps the novice become a better archer himself. I have shot with more than a few national champion archers, and boy, it has been an education. When participating with good shooters, the novice shouldn't cringe but take advantage of the opportunity by observing, listening, and pondering. It makes sense that if one is going to take advice and pattern his shooting from someone else, it should be from an archer who is successful rather than a pal who is still learning himself.

One of the best sights at traditional contests is watching all the homemade equipment. Bows, arrows, and leather goods created by the contestants themselves are always in abundance. I never tire of seeing the myriad of homespun back quivers.

For someone who is coming into the sport, the traditional archery shoot is an excellent place to buy a used bow from a vendor or another archer. This allows him to purchase an inexpensive starter bow. Then, after he becomes more proficient, he may choose to buy a custom bow at another shoot from a fine bowyer.

I met a great bowyer at the Great Lakes longbow shoot in 1986. At the time he was fairly new at bowmaking. He introduced himself as Gus Dellaghelfa. We struck up an instant friendship and now usually shoot together yearly at some traditional shoot or another. Over the years, his bows have become absolutely top-notch and so has his friendship. He really likes to give me a bad time, and I love to reciprocate. A few years ago we were shooting together in Michigan. One target was shot from a perch in a tree. The deer target was down on the ground at about 30 yards. I shot first and noticed a large tree about halfway and to the left of the target. One had to shoot somewhat straight to keep from striking that tree. I made a good shot and grinned at ol' Gus as he stepped up to shoot. When he got ready to draw, I asked him, "What kinda tree is that in front of the target, Gus?" He mumbled something and drew his arrow and shot it directly into that tree. I nearly fell down laughing. He flashed me one of his hundred dollar smiles, because he perceived the humor in it, and also he offered a stern warning that he would mete out his revenge. This sort of thing makes for great fun and grand memories.

I have some friends here in my home state that cause me all kinds of problems at shoots. The only way to describe these guys is simply that they are "bad company"—definitely the kind of fellows that a loving mother warns her son about. I do not hesitate to tell you their names in warning perchance you should run across one of 'em. There's Steve Gorr, who fancies himself as a shooter; George Meier, whose main purpose, as the eldest, is to correct all the misinformation I've gleaned about archery; and Cecil McConnell, whose calling is to laugh at my shooting and let me know what a fool I am. As for me, I've always tried to be a regular fellow and help the boys. I occasionally deliberately miss a target that Steve hits, so his ego won't be damaged. I always ask George the correct way to nock an arrow, because that is the only skill he has. I do cute little things that embarrass Cecil so that he can tell me what a fool I am. When the four of us

Steve Gorr excels on targets and game with his '3 fingers under' draw.

get together, we are so rowdy and irreverent that others shooting with us find it traumatic. Deep down, we really like each other and delight in our shooting sessions. I have noticed that many archers have the same fun with their friends at traditional events.

During the 1950's and 1960's I enjoyed going to traditional archery shoots. With the advent of the compound, in the late 1960's, the complexion of the sport really changed. By 1980, it was about impossible to find a formal gathering of traditional archers in America; but by the mid 1980's, the traditional shoots started blooming again. Now they are a common occurrence. Most states have traditional associations that can assist a person in finding the times and locations of their shoots.

From my observations, archers and compounders don't mix too well at shoots. One reason is that the compound clubs often set the targets at longer distances, and this is not realistic for most traditional shooters. Another is that compounders sometimes believe that they shoot superior equipment, and therefore reflect this in their attitudes. Hard core traditionalists don't consider compounding as archery, so they deem compounders as interlopers in the sport. Whether all of this is right or wrong, I'll let you decide. But, from my perspective, I believe that generally the traditional bowman is more comfortable at shoots where the compound does not participate.

When the hot sun bites through the summer sky and compels us to go out and play, the traditional archery events are places where we bowmen rendezvous to participate and enjoy the pleasure of companionship with others endowed with the time-honored archer's heart.

Another stump bites the dust.

Chapter 12
ALONE

During a year's time, I build up quite a collection of mismatched arrows. Some come from sets used for target practice and others from those used at shoots. Quite often, these arrows have had a broken point and then have been repaired with a blunt-head. At any rate, I have an accumulation. Near the end of each summer, when the grass is brown and the days are lazy, I pack up these arrows with a couple bows and head into the rugged Olympic Mountains in the northwest corner of Washington state. This area is fairly near to my home. The center of the region contains the Olympic National Park, and surrounding it is a national forest. Throughout the national forest are many dirt logging roads. All alone, I assail the region for two or three days in search of adventure and solitude.

One of my first stops is a huge meadow. About 200 yards out into the meadow is an ancient giant of a snag that once was a towering Douglas fir. I launch a few arrows until I make a good hit. What a delight it is to see a well cast shaft sing its way up in the sky and curve down and strike the old snag with a resounding thump!

My course continues many miles up a narrow valley with steep, craggy, alpine peaks on each side. At one place I park the truck and climb up on a flat rock and glass the peaks for mountain goats. One can spend hours watching these white, alpine ghosts. The fresh air and warm sun eventually lulls me into a peaceful slumber. These snoozes are unlike those experienced at home. They are completely refreshing and relaxing.

While sitting on my mountain perch, I cannot help but be struck by the beauties of nature. My thoughts are taken to the master architect of all this beauty, Skookum Tyee Sahalie, the powerful Chief from above. I sit there and give reverent glory to His name and the bounties He has blest me with—especially being allowed to commune with Him in His great outdoor cathedral, to ponder His mighty works and our relationship.

Overlooking the valley, I feel the urge to see how far I can shoot an arrow. Picking a couple of my poorest shafts, I launch them as far as possible. I wonder, in all of that wilderness, if they will ever be seen by the human eye again. But what about the eye of a "bigfoot?" This is supposedly the heart of "Sasquatch" country! But, alas, I've never seen one, even though I've spent most of a lifetime out here.

Way out in the middle of nowhere, I have found a region with outstanding stumps among huge fir trees. I drive to this place and pick out a quiver full of arrows. The rest of the afternoon is spent in a solitary assault on the stumps. I wind my way through the forest from stump to stump. Each stump offers a fresh target. If I miss, lose, or break an arrow, what do I care? I have plenty more! Sometimes I carry my plant identification guide to help learn the different plant species I happen across. You may understand how therapeutic it is being secluded from other human beings in a natural setting.

By the late afternoon, I slowly drive along the hillside logging roads overlooking clear-cut areas. Occasionally, I spy a big blacktail buck or two out on their evening rounds. The season won't open for a month, and I note in my mind to come back then. Black bears can be spotted in the far off clear-cuts looking for huckleberries and other tidbits. It is interesting to blow the predator call and watch their reactions.

I have found a flat area way up high on a hillside that makes a good campsite. It faces the east and what a marvelous view. The panorama, on a clear day, exposes Mt. Rainier, Mt. St. Helens, and Mt. Adams standing in their stately glory. I lay out my sleeping bag and start a small fire to warm the soul more than anything else. Just after dark, I can find several satellites crossing the starry heavens. Laying back in my cozy nest, I turn a baseball game on the transistor radio. With a bag of corn chips, I spend a pleasureful, secluded evening.

There is a place I'd like to take all traditional archers. It is near where I camp. The winding dirt road descends very quickly. At one point, near the top, you can look almost straight down and see where the road snakes along about 300 yards beneath. The road down below makes an excellent target! Hardly a traveler uses this old logging road, and if he did, you could see him from way off. So, it is safe to shoot down at the road—not safe for arrows though. If you should shoot too far, they will be swallowed up in a thick, hillside forest. If you don't shoot far enough, the arrows will be lost on a steep, mountain slope. The only place to hit is right on the narrow road itself.

Imagine standing at the edge of a mountain side, and way down the hill in front you see a tiny road. You nock an arrow and take your best flight-shooting stance. The fresh, morning mountain breeze whips across your face. You pull the stout cord until anchor is reached, and instantaneously you cast the shaft high out into the sky in a parabolic curve. The arrow now starts to dive steeply down. Down it goes, almost as hard to follow as a memory. And then, way down on the road, you detect a slight puff of dust, and a mere split second later you hear the faintest delayed thud. But, friend, it is oh so hard to shoot but one arrow. You must try it again and again. Like some overpowering addiction, you are compelled to shoot until your quiver is emptied.

The ride down the steep road is twisty and slow until you come to the spot where your arrows are.

My next stop is an evergreen swamp that is the home of a rather large elk herd. It is also the home of some nice stumps. Often while stump shooting there, I find the herd. It is always exciting to stalk and observe Roosevelt elk. I have learned from these escapades that blowing my predator call can make them real angry. They will charge all around my hiding place with hackles raised looking for the varmint that is hurting one of their calves.

Once I found a giant old cedar tree that anciently had blown over near the swamp. Red cedar is very resistant to decomposition. Under this fall down, I found an opening of about six square feet. I could see bear hair hanging from the hole. I took off my quiver, and with a small flashlight, I crawled into the opening. Inside was a real neat bear lodge. The main top portion was hollowed out in the tree. The floor was dried leaves and other duff. It was about five feet high, five feet wide, and twelve feet long. Bear hair was everywhere, and so was a sharp, musty odor. Obviously, blackbear have been using this place as a "Hibernation Hilton" for decades. When I crawled out, I had goose flesh. What an eerie place! I have often thought about coming back on a cold, winter day.

Stump shooting in this area is a joy. There are many old stumps everywhere. They are soft and spongy. People are scarce. Many birds greet the archer's eye, including an abundance of ospreys and bald eagles. Game abounds.

Often my next stop is a small café. After a day or two of roughing it, us mountain men like to come out of the hills and rendezvous at a local eatery for civilized food. There is a particular one on this trip. I don't know its name, but I call it "Cholesterol Heaven." Now, this part of my journey can hold the most adventure. When I walk into the establishment in my "mountain man" outfit, every eye in the joint fixes on me. Most of these eyes belong to loggers. Loggers hang around these "greasy spoon" places. They like to talk to each other in roaring voices. Whenever a stranger comes in, they become quiet as mice and give hard stares at the wayfarer.

I belly up to the counter, and the waitress attends to my order. I order eggs, hash browns, sausage, and toast. She says, "Do you want the regular order or 'Hefty Man' order?" Everyone is waiting for my reply.

"Why, I want 'Hefty Man' of course!" With that, everyone nods their approval. I may be okay after all. When the meal comes, there is enough food to feed me for a week, but I dig in enthusiastically. After I finish my last agonizing bite and am wondering if my colon will be able to survive the oily onslaught, a logger sitting next to me asks what I've been doing out in his part of the woods. I tell him about my bow and arrow, and he gets very interested. He tells his chums, and soon everyone has a bow and arrow story. We all talk for awhile and then depart friends. It always amazes me how people have a natural liking for archery.

That evening finds me camped in a forest of old alder. A little stream runs jauntily by. Bats race about in search of flying insects. As darkness settles, I can hear the hoots of several owls in the distance. If I am clever, I can hoot back and get a response.

On the morrow, I rise and head home. Most of my arrows are lost or broken. What a worthy way to use them up! I have a storehouse of memories and a renewed spirit.

Fellow archer, I wrote this section to let you know that there are many facets to our sport. Most areas of our country have places for us to get away for a day or so to explore, shoot, and commune with ourselves in the wondrous outdoors.

Champion Michigan archer of the 1940's and 50's, Harold Doan.

Chapter 13
THE GREAT LAWN GAME

European history for centuries, has told of the great archery events held all over the continent on shooting greens. Well-heeled ladies and gentlemen loved the sport. Magnificent contests were held, and large social gatherings accompanied these events. Even the touted Robin Hood was lured out of hiding to participate at one such competition.

America did not go untouched. After the Civil War, lawn target archery clubs sprang up all over the eastern half of the country, largely from the efforts of Will Thompson. Target archery stayed very popular in the U.S. until the mid-1970's when the compound came upon the scene.

Traditional target archery should be part of every worthy bowman's repertoire. But what is a person to do? A target range takes up a great deal of space. Once common in city parks, the target range has disappeared because of accident liability worries and lack of interest. Local archery clubs are hesitant to put them up because everyone is into the 3-D, trail shoot fad. I personally believe that if traditional archery clubs and organizations would set up target ranges and competitions, a lot of good would come. Critics of this idea may say that this would just drive some of the hunting archers away and a class system would appear, segregating the good shooters from the poor shooters. It might be claimed that the hunting style of shooting just is not conducive to the target game. There is a flavor of truth to all this, but what we do now makes us one dimensional.

Traditional archery, as it is practiced in the early 1990's, is very one-dimensional. Hunting is the driving force. All practice seems to be done to make a person a better hunting shot. Archery events are usually hunting oriented with animal targets. The hunting bow and the hunting arrow dominate the equipment selection. I have friends who shoot only their hunting bows and hunting weight arrows at short hunting distances. Isn't that a real kick? Being so single-minded, they never learn the joy of shooting a good group at 70 yards.

I am very fortunate to live on three acres of property. I have put in a two-target lawn range that gives me practice up to 70 yards. The range is level and planted with clover. Fruit trees and flowers adorn it. On warm summer evenings, it is pleasant to go out and practice. Shooting several ends of six arrows each at 60 yards helps build a consistency in form, especially with a hunting bow.

Having access to a target range allows me to objectively evaluate my shooting accuracy. One popular target round is called the "American Round." It consists of shooting ends of six arrows each—five ends starting at 60 yards, five ends at 50 yards, and five ends at 40 yards at the standard 48" target face. The scoring on the standard target face has changed over the last few decades, and I recommend using the more classical scoring for each arrow. That is; gold = 9 points, red = 7 points, blue = 5 points, black = 3 points, and white = 1 point. By scoring this way, one can compare himself with the past masters.

When I shoot at the target game my stance changes a little. I stand more upright and more perpendicular to the target. I do not use sight pins, because that takes some of the human element out of it, and also that would not give me an accurate gauge to judge myself against the earlier, traditional, target masters. I do use modern composite bow construction, which is definitely better. Therefore, I give myself a minus handicap on an American Round.

Often a new toxophilite will ask himself, "Am I a good enough shooter to proceed into the sylvan vale to hunt the wily deer?" Art Young and Saxton Pope are considered hunting masters. Pope stated that his best practice American Round was 538, and Art Young's best was 626. This gives one a standard to shoot for. Pope and Young used yew target bows in the 50-pound range and wooden target arrows. So go forth and give it a try yourself. Use traditional equipment and try to get into the spirit of it. I believe that when a person can shoot 500 or better, he is becoming a pretty good shooter.

Howard Hill participated in target archery. As with most archers of his time, he loved to put on his tournament white clothing and go to the greens to shoot and enjoy the companionship of other archers. One fellow told me that he witnessed Hill shooting at 100 yards at a southern California range. A side wind was blowing so strongly that, at that range, the others could not keep their arrows in the butts. Uncannily, Hill kept his in the target. By the way, Hill said that his best American Round was 684. What's the point of all this? Well, to me it means that even though target shooting is a different game than hunting, an archer can benefit from and enjoy both.

Recently, I was feeling the weight of the world on my shoulders. There were many things on my mind—most of them negative. You probably know the feeling. Well, on this day, I had an hour to spare, so I went out to my range. My shooting had not been the best, I had missed an easy shot at a deer a couple of days earlier. I started my practice at 30 yards and then decided to try an end at 60 yards. I went back and shot five arrows in the gold and one arrow in the red. I collected my arrows and went back to the house. For the rest of the day the glow of the great group lifted my spirits.

Target archery is really for us who love to shoot arrows. From my earliest days, when I first launched a feathered shaft, until now, I never, ever tire of shooting arrows. Target archery lets us shoot lots of arrows with a purpose.

Every year I am fortunate enough to go to several traditional shoots. I like them very much. At most, there is a cock-o'-the-walk or two that struts around and proclaims how great a shooter he is. I find no fault with this, but some of these people are deceived. They are not proven on a target range. I would like to see very traditional target competitions set up in conjunction with these shoots. I'll bet you that a better class of shooter would emerge if one was forced to shoot 90 arrows or so at fixed distances.

Robin Hood, Will Thompson, Maurice Thompson, Art Young, Fred Bear, and Howard Hill are all great archers of the past that loved and excelled at the lawn game.

Author's best field archery form under the olive trees in 1959.

Chapter 14

ARROWSHOOTING

As a nine year old, I had a strong loving feeling for my family. Most all of my joy came from my parents and older brothers and sister. Therefore on this magnificent summer day, I was beside myself with happiness and anticipation. The family was leaving for a long weekend in the mountains. We were going to stay in a cabin and do all sorts of marvelous things. I had about two hours to wait while things got piled into the cars. My best friend, Jack Wilson, came by the house with his new bow and arrow set. He wanted to know if I would like to go out to the side yard and shoot with him. We set up a cardboard box as a target and started to shoot at it. I discovered then what a thrilling thing it is to shoot arrows. Up to this time, my mother was not fond of bows and arrows, sling-shots, or BB guns. They could hurt a little boy or put his eye out. When she saw me shooting arrows out in the yard, she called, "Remember, we're leaving in about an hour, so don't plan on being out there too long and be careful!" But the time flew by, and I had to leave. I can still recall wanting to take just one more shot while my family threatened to abandon me if I didn't get into the car.

There is an addiction that comes with shooting arrows. Most people, however, never get it. Maybe shooting arrows can be likened to drinking alcohol. A majority can take a drink or two and leave it alone. Some folks feel a strong need to drink only on occasion. And others are so compelled, that their lives are completely ruled by this drug.

I am one of those people whose life has been taken over by shooting arrows—I just can't get enough of it. There are others like me. This addiction has caused grief at times, like when my dad drove me to the field archery range and said, "I'll pick you up at four o'clock sharp. Be here in the parking lot then." Four o'clock found me up on target 20, having a great old time slinging arrows. When I came back an hour later, my dad decided that for a long while, he would not chauffeur me to the range and back.

Right after I was married, I dropped my wife off at church to do some work for a social or some such. She told me to pick her up in a couple of hours. I set off to the field range and came back three hours later. Now, you wouldn't think that one measly hour would mean that much, but it did. I really got the what for.

As a young man, I realized that I had a problem with this arrowshooting addiction, so I set off to do something about it. I heard of a group that helped people with addictions. It was called "AA" (Arrowshooters Anonymous). I went to a meeting. Several people were there. I recognized a number of them and, quite frankly, I felt somewhat embarrassed about being there and laying bare my darkest secrets openly. I was given a mentor to help me over the rough times ahead. I was to call him when struck with the wild urge to recklessly abandon common sense and go out arrowshooting. But he turned out to be more rotten than me. We ended up going on a "Lost Weekend" shooting binge, and it nearly cost us our marriages.

This fellow had a bigger problem than me. One weekend he went on a wild fling. It started on Saturday and ended Tuesday. On Tuesday he came home to confess to his wife his sins. He said, "Honey, I want to be perfectly honest with you. Saturday, I went to a bar and met a beautiful brunette. We danced a little and ended up at her apartment. Sunday, I felt so bad about what I'd done, that I went over to the bar to have a drink to build my courage to tell you, but I met this pretty redhead and ended up at her house that night. Monday, I was down in the dumps and went to the bar to drown myself in sorrow for being so unfaithful; but I met this gorgeous blond, and one thing led to another, and I woke up in her apartment this morning feeling so guilty that I decided to come home immediately and plead to you for forgiveness and to promise I won't go out carousing again." His wife glared at him and said, "You can't fool me with that malarkey, Harry! You've been out arrowshooting!"

What separates a real archer from the common everyday bowhunter is the former's addiction to shooting arrows. Here

124

are some examples: One friend of mine had to drive two hours to get to a shoot. He was so excited that he stopped the car after an hour to shoot some arrows at stumps along the way. Another guy I know claims he is an avid bowhunter. He goes hunting all the time, but seldom does he go places just to sling arrows.

Do you remember the story of Robin Hood? What about how he died? You may recall that old Robin was poisoned, and he knew he was a goner. So what does he do? Well, here was a great arrowshoot'n addict. He called for his bow and arrow. He placed his arrow on the string and said, "Where my arrow lands, make it my grave." And he up and flinged his last arrow. What a way to go, eh?

One retired sailor friend carried his longbow-and-arrows aboard ship. Whenever the ship docked, he would seek out a local archery range. While his buddies would be ashore raising hell, he would be off somewhere arrowshooting. He now has many pleasant memories of shooting at places all around the globe.

A new acquaintance of mine wanted to go stump-shooting with me. We made arrangements, and he arrived at the appointed time. He had eight arrows in his quiver. "Where's your arrows?" I ask.

"Here in my quiver," he replied.

"Is that all you brought?" I queried in surprise.

"Yeah, I'm careful with them," he responded. It was a boring outing. This guy wouldn't shoot at any stump where he might loose or damage an arrow. Not all archers are arrowshooters. If you are an arrowshooter, don't be surprised by some who are not. It may be best just to avoid them.

Probably the worst thing an arrowshooter can do, however, is to over-bow himself, because this limits the number of shots he can take. I've been selling bows for years, and I find it puzzling why a person will pay hundreds of dollars for a bow that he can only accurately shoot 20 arrows from before becoming tired.

There's a 14-year-old student at my school here. He is a member of the Society for Creative Anachronism. This national group loves to reenact medieval life. They have great times, and one of their main sports is archery—usually tournament archery. This boy just took a big growing spurt, and I ask him if he got a new bow yet. He said he hadn't, but really needed a bigger one. I asked what weight he was looking for. He replied that a 35-to 40-pound bow was what he wanted. He explained that, with this weight, he could shoot all day without getting tired out. I marveled to myself that this young man has more wisdom than the majority of adult archers that I know. When he said this, I smiled because I knew he was already a real arrowshooter.

Arrowshooters don't store their arrows in boxes. They have them handy in quivers and other places. I have a large barrel in my den where I keep several dozen arrows. That way I can grab a handful of the type I want, and set off to do some shooting.

Arrowshooters usually enjoy rabbit hunting because of all the shooting action. I have hunted in places in California that provided hours and hours of constant shooting at ground squirrels, cotton-tails, jackrabbits, quail, and other small game. Carp shooting often provides similar shooting opportunities. Contrast this with big-game hunting, where it is possible to end the season with only one shot.

Old Cecil is coming by today. He's made a new longbow and wants me to shoot it. He's an arrowshooter and has all the familiar weaknesses. When he shows up, he will have several dozen arrows with him. We'll go up to my target, and I'll be able to shoot his arrows. I just love shooting other guys' arrows.

We have a running dialog while shooting. It goes like this: "Watch me hit that deer on the left in the heart." Twang.

"Yeah, since when was its heart over there. Now, watch me!" Twang.

"That's a good shot."

"You bet it's a good shot, old man. Someday I'll teach you how I do it."

"Oh, yeah! Let's see if you can beat this arrow, Bristle-Face." Twang.

"OK, watch this." Twang.

"Well there's a broken arrow if I've ever seen one. Watch and tell me if this arrow is fishtailing." Twang.

"Yeah, it did. Better raise the brace height." And this same jargon may go on for an hour or two, because arrowshooters just naturally behave this way. As the world travels it course in the universe, as events shape the land, as wars are fought, as kings and rulers come and go, we arrowshooters will be out somewhere flinging arrows and letting our worldly concerns disappear like a far-flung shaft over an alpine canyon.

THE BOWMAN

The bowman pauses as he treks across a snowy alpine slope. He surveys the rugged peaks, valleys, and streams. By gosh, there is nothing that he can't traverse! The outdoors is his home. He has all the vigor, strength, and knowledge to proceed through it as a free agent.

In his hand is a stout bow fashioned by his own skill. He has taken much game with this weapon, and his ability on targets is excellent. Yes, he has met many challenges afield with success.

Oh, bowman, wouldn't it be wonderful to tramp across all of the earth's game fields? You are definitely up to the task. Only if there were more time! Only if there were more money! Remember, there is a young family depending on you at home. Well, for now, the mountains of home will do just fine.

Look up on that hillside, bowman. Isn't that a herd of deer? It's only an hour's hike, so make some tracks and go get 'em!

Great old Oregon archer, Chester Stevenson.

Section III

HUNTING

"Old Chief" My favorite
hunting horse in 1934
Walt Wilhelm

Chapter 15

TRADITIONAL BOWHUNTING:

Becoming One With Nature

How each person expresses his hunting desire varies; some shoot rifles, some use shotguns, some like muzzle-loaders, some enjoy compounds, some use archery, and some prefer a combination of any of these. Why a person chooses one weapon over another is a mystery. Being that we are addressing traditional archery, how is it different in its hunting approach than the modern expressions of contemporary bowhunting? Generally speaking, the traditionalists place more value on acquiring and using techniques that are centered on physical and mental prowess. This requires a knowledge of stalking skills, animal behavior, woodcraft, and self-sufficiency.

You'll never find a deserving bowman of the traditional creed riding in a vehicle around the hills, road-hunting for game. This is a cheap thrill. A few seasons back, I was invited to hunt a late season deer area with three fine hunters. I had not hunted this part of the Blue Mountains before, but the others had. They assured me that there would be plenty of deer for those willing to climb to the tops of the hills for them. Well, for three days we dogged up those snow-laden mountains, and I've rarely ever had such fine hunting. The strange thing was that everyday, after getting back to camp, we would talk to several bowhunters of the contemporary persuasion who complained about not seeing any deer. Everyone in my party filled their tags. The problem was that the others simply wouldn't leave the luxury of their vehicles for more than an hour or two. This is not an isolated event, I've seen similar scenarios played many times.

The traditional archer learns his hunting by experiencing nature; the more he experiences it, the more natural he becomes. It is often a hard adjustment to go into the wilds after spending the daily existence in the confines of modern society. It is a temptation to take the shrouds of civilization to the outdoors with us, but this is not our mode. Sometimes it takes me as much as four or five days before my outing feels comfortable. Then I start reverting to the wilderness way quickly. Several archers of my acquaintance camp in Indian teepees. Let me not leave the reader with the impression that one has to be an aboriginal to enjoy the sport. (But haven't we all longed to be one at some time?) I'm just advocating that the acquisition of outdoor skills will not only make the jaunt more comfortable, safer, and fill the game-bag, but it will provide more satisfying rewards for those endowed with the hunter's heart. Nature has a place for the archer that goes afield prepared in the manner of the traditionalist, because she finds that his unsophistication inherently molds him to her bosom.

To learn this, a wise novice picks a home hunting ground area and perfects it. In most areas, a rabbit patch could be ideal for this. They are usually accessible, teach the fundamentals of stalking, provide shooting practice on game, and this is just plain fun.

Later, the hunter will want to chase larger game. I am a firm believer that every bowman should develop one or two deer areas that are reasonably nearby and become an expert on these grounds. From there on, the hunter may go forth among all game fields if his inclination and purse dictate.

I've found most folks that take up the traditional way of hunting archery are not out to slay a large quantity of beasts. Quantity connotes egotism, and this calls for impressing others with your feats. The hunting archer is looking for intrinsic rewards. The hunt, to him, means a personal, private, simple contest between the game and the hunter. The personal contest is heightened by the closeness required to encounter the game animal. A good hunter knows his effective accuracy range and doesn't sling arrows willy-nilly at animals.

There seems to be a concept going forth throughout the outdoor sports (hunting and fishing) that to be worthy, one must bag a large quantity, or large sizes, of fish and game. This idea is pervading archery—mainly from commercial sources, and often tempts the hunter into taking ill-advised long shots. Real hunters discipline themselves in their selection of shots at game.

For many of us, traditional archery hunting is a social sport. Some of the most educational and enjoyable aspects of the hunt occur in fraternal conferences long before the actual hunting takes place. On occasion, often during the most dreary winter evenings, a gathering of traditional bowmen will take place in some archer's cozy, warm den. Much information is passed from bowman to bowman. At times like this a novice is initiated by the experienced concerning such things as taking only proper shots, respect for game, the true meaning of the hunt, and effective equipment. While a storm rages outside, a light-hearted storm brews inside among the bowmen regarding the correct shape of a broadhead, the best hunting weight bow, the ideal length of fletching, or whose bow is the fastest. Refreshments are past around and so are the lies. Peals of laughter ring out as the story of the host falling out his tree-stand is retold. The T.V. is turned on, and a video explains how to call and hunt the Rocky Mountain elk. Next comes serious discussion on where everyone will hunt in the fall. More hyperbole spews forth. Discussions go late into the night, then the participants go happily home. These get-togethers are an important phase of the hunt.

Another part of the hunt is the quality of the outdoor experience that is readily available to most traditional archers.

I drove off the ferry onto Orcas Island in Washington state's San Juan Islands. It was ten o'clock, and the Indian summer morning was already warming up. A charming thirty minute drive to the other side of the island brought me to my hunting area. My objective was to bag one of the island (blacktail) deer that are numerous on the San Juans.

Orcas Island is dotted with quaint farms, residences, a beautiful state park, and lots of "no trespassing" signs. The island is a typical example of what is happening all across the country. With increasing human population, more good hunting territories are being eaten up by man's rural encroachment.

I parked my car and marveled at the striking colors of the deciduous foliage as a signal of impending cold. I took out my

67-inch hunting bow and hip-quiver. I spied a soft stump and shot a few blunts into it to sharpen my eye. As I pulled out the arrows, I was reminded of another time when this same stump provided some heated competition with a couple of my pals. I lost and had to provide supper.

Hunting the small deer on Orcas is very similar to hunting farmland whitetails. They know every bush and pocket in their territory. Realizing this, I checked the wind direction and carefully plotted my course. My hunt would take me through several stands of firs, along a ridge of deciduous trees, and then out to a weedy clearing.

With complete enjoyment, I made my way on the selected course. This is my favorite method of hunting. Ever so slowly, I stalked from cover to cover searching for telltale signs of deer ... a movement here or a color or strange line there. I looked at the sky and noticed that the sun was beating down strongly, signifying mid-day. "Well, I guess I ought to go see if some lunch can be rounded up," I said succumbing to one of my weaknesses.

I still had the clearing to hunt, and I approached it carefully. Then I froze. 80 yards away were two browsing deer at the edge of an overgrown logging road. The range was too far for a decent shot. Slowly, I worked my way across the clearing to less than 30 yards. I watched the nearest deer, a doe, walk away to feed on a succulent bush. This made the other deer nervous, and he started to trot toward some cover.

There comes a moment when the experienced archer knows that it is time to shoot. I raised my bow, concentrated on the deer's ribs, allowed for its travel, and turned the arrow loose. The shaft sped over the tops of the knee-high vegetation. Chunk! It buried behind the last rib. The deer bolted and did a strange thing. It ran at top speed making a semi-circle that would bring it within fifteen yards of me! I swung my bow up and loosed another shaft that caught the deer in the neck. Down it went.

Why am I telling you this story? Well, certainly not to prove my hunting prowess. I can relate several more tales of being unsuccessful. What I want to point out is the quality of hunting that traditional archery allows. On this hunt, it took a degree of skill to find and stalk, to within shooting range, a wary deer. This method of shooting the bow not only proved to be the best but also required learned and practiced skills. The real clincher was the thrill of watching the flight of the arrow as it sought out its target. Place this with the fact that I searched out my home state's hunting grounds to find the area of the hunt. Add this all together and you get an activity that no other shooting sport can claim.

I remember a cold December day a few seasons ago on a high Cascade Mountain ridge. The wind was gusting through the draws and biting at my ears and nose. Ice had frozen into tiny balls at the ends of the hairs that protruded from under my hunting hat. Rigorous activity that only mountain hunting can give had caused the sweat to collect and then freeze on my hair. My legs hurt from propelling me up and down the ridges and draws all morning. I scanned across a hillside and spied a movement. It was my faithful hunting partner. I caught his attention, and he ambled up to me. "Hey, you clod, I could see you a mile away. No wonder every deer in the county knows you're here!" I greeted him in a friendly fashion.

He grinned and replied, "I see you are still standing about in one place...probably think'n more 'bout food than deer."

We retreated under a large ponderosa pine to have lunch and lounge around before the afternoon hunt. "Isn't this fun?" I asked. Here we were, miles away from anywhere, snow and wind blowing up a gale, enjoying food we'd normally turn our noses up at, dog tired, our peers at home watching a pro-football game by warm hearths, and both of us loving every minute of it.

"You know, most people would say we're nuts!" he replied.

A rotten television documentary on hunting came to my mind. It portrayed hunters as slobs who enjoyed easy hunts and killing tame, pinned-up animals. As I looked around, I wished that the same TV network would objectively capture some of the hunts participated in by other traditional bowmen and myself. We most certainly are not in the sport for ease or the blood-letting desire. We enjoy taking game, but that is only one

137

part of it. I believe we archers enjoy the total experience of being out in nature and in some way being innocent and pure.

I studied my partner, a man who has spent most of his recreational time in the woods. Fine snow was falling over him, and the freezing wind was making a crimson kiss on his ears. He didn't care. He was in his element. He was scanning a ridge above his favorite canyon. I knew it wouldn't be long until he would be migrating to its environs. "Well, old horse, I'll be off...see you at camp tonight," he said. I've had the pleasure of knowing many traditional bowmen. Practically all of them are very independent. They have thorough knowledge of their weapons, and they can use them effectively. They have deep feelings for nature, and are no strangers to a cold wind, a hot plain, a pine-scented forest, the call of the loon, the intoxicating freshness of a sunrise on an alpine crest, or the wonders of the Great Spirit. Their craft is unencumbered by the vast quantities of technological devices created to give them an advantage over their quarry. With their own wits and basic skills, they enter the wilds in unsophisticated harmony. As stewards of the outdoors, they are vigilant in maintaining their heritage and are actively involved with programs that insure it will be preserved for the generations to come.

Chapter 16

THERAPY OF THE HILLS

Years ago, Washington state had a very large, archery only, hunting area in a wilderness area of the Cascade Mountains. The Cascades are rugged and stunning. Jewel-like alpine lakes are dotted all over the region along with fish-filled creeks and rivers. Deer, elk, goats, mountain lions, and bear abounded in the area along with numerous small game. A valley ran between the high peaks. A beautiful creek rambled through the pristine valley. A wonderful camping spot was next to the roaring creek.

The season lasted from September through the end of December. Several of my friends and I loved to bivouac there. We would set up our tents and then proceed to make a real archer's camp.

Early in the crisp mornings, we'd arise to the tantalizing aroma of a hunter's breakfast. One fellow always wanted to be up beforehand to do this chore. It intrigues me how wonderful cooking bacon smells in the outdoors. We would pack our stomachs and then shoot a few arrows into our practice target. Then off we would depart in a myriad of directions to slay the mighty stag. Some would stay low in the valley looking for the resident deer; others would ascend to the high meadows looking for the elusive alpine bucks; and still others would take fishing rods and set out for wild native rainbow and Dolly Varden trout. Occasionally one of us might have a goat tag and climb the peaks looking for the white goats.

The camp would always be deserted in the late afternoon, but just before dark the hunters would start trickling back. Sometimes there would be a deer hanging from the game pole; but more often than not, the hunters would show up with great tales of the day's adventure. The evening meal might consist of juicy, roasted, venison chunks dipped into chili salsa; or maybe our meal would be savory stew, fried trout, or grilled burgers. Whatever the fare, we'd wolf it down with great gusto, because a hunter just can't troop around the Cascades without acquiring a gigantic appetite.

The camp would glow with light from the gasoline lanterns and the dancing pow-wow fire. The day's arrows would be resharpened and necessary repairs accomplished. Occasionally a chilling, primal howl could be heard echoing from the slopes. Conversation would start up. One fellow might tell of the long-haired, cinnamon bear that he followed all morning but couldn't quite get a shot at. A hunter would tell of walking under a bobcat in a tree, another would relate missing an easy shot at a doe down by the bridge. One would pipe up and say that he was a buck-hunter not a doe-hunter. A few good natured barbs would ensue. Maybe it's because I'm such a social person, but what a marvelous experience it is to sit around a campfire with several companions of various occupational, educational, religious, racial, and philosophical backgrounds and share our wisdom and escapades. Some of my best memories come from this campfire camaraderie. Hunting archers who do not participate in these kinds of activities are missing out on one of the best parts of the chase.

Tired from the day's activities, the hunters would migrate to their beds. Thoughts of the morrow's adventures would fight their way through their minds; sleepiness and comfort pushing them out. A blissful rest would fall upon our camp. A light stream of campfire smoke drifted into the starry heavens, and a great gray owl hooted his wild call while the hunters dreamed, restfully awaiting the dawn to bring another day of joy.

Chapter 17

THEM THERE GOATS

I want the reader to know right here and now that I am not the greatest of nimrods, but a passion for the hunt runs through me. Take mountain goats for example, I've tried, without success, to get one for nearly 30 years. The only thing that has happened is that they made a complete goat out of me.

Around 1972, my friend Jerry and I were each drawn for our first goat tags. As with good hunters, we decided to do a little scouting of the area before hunting season. To get to the region where we planned to do goat mayhem, we had to first travel six miles up a steep, mountain trail. This, in itself, was a three hour hike. Ah, but Jerry suggested that we take his trail motorcycle. I would ride on the back. It turned out to be a bruising mistake. When we reached our destination, I sorely dismounted and vowed not to ever ride that thing again.

After our sortie scouting for goats on the craggy peaks, Jerry and I met at the bike to go back down the trail, I declined the offer to ride and opted to walk. He said that would be fine, because he could do a little trout fishing while he waited.

As I started my shank's mare journey down the trail, I could hear his little bike buzzing down the forest ahead. Then I heard the popping of his .22 pistol. "Guess old Jerry shot us a grouse," I told myself upon hearing the gunfire. When we were scouting he always packed his .22 for such purposes. I continued down the trail.

A couple of hundred yards further on, Jerry came frantically running up to me. "Shoot a grouse?" I asked. Then I ascertained there was something bothering him.

"A bear charged out after my bike!" he puffed.

"Uh, you didn't shoot 'im with the .22, did you?"

"Yes...this bear's crazy!" he puffed. I couldn't believe Jerry tried to take on a bear with a little .22 .

"Well, where's the bear? Did you kill 'im?"

"He's back down the trail, and he's mad as all get out!" Jerry told me with a wild look in his eye. I glanced down the trail, and here came the bear some 40 yards away bounding towards us. Now, I wasn't too afraid, because Jerry was a little portly, and I knew I could outrun him. I figured that if the bear was out to perform carnage, he'd do it on Jerry. So I started streaking back up the trail with Jerry following. After a bit, we whirled around and looked for the bruin. He was nowhere in sight.

We tarried for awhile and decided to go back down to the bike. When we reached it, Mr. Bear couldn't be seen. We figured we'd seen the last of him. Wrong! Fifteen yards away, the bear jumped up out of some bushes on his hind legs. Angrily he yelled and leaped on a nearby tree, pulling bark from it like a chainsaw. Jerry and I stood frozen in fear. The bear growled and stood erect again gazing at us. He had a white patch on his chest, and I could see Jerry standing next to me pointing his pistol. The bear let out an awful growl, and I yelled, "Shoot!..Shoot, Jerry, shoot!" Jerry didn't. Obviously the bear was furious.

I figured it was now time for me to retreat back up the mountain and let the bear deal with Jerry. As I spun to go, Jerry wasn't beside me! He had zipped off without my knowing it while my focus was transfixed on the bruin. Jerry was 40 yards up the hill. At that moment, I broke the world record for the 40-yard dash! For the next few minutes, we could hear the angry bear ripping and breaking brush below us. After a long time, we sneaked back to the motorcycle and buzzed out of there.

Later, after hunting season opened, I talked to a fellow who killed an aggressive bear in the same area with his bow and arrow.

I rose really early on the opening of goat season so as to be in the peaks right after daylight. The sun had crept over the crests revealing a beautiful, crisp, cold alpine morning. I was ambling quietly along a ridge when I heard the explosive sounds of rocks being dislodged and rolling down a slope above and in front of me. There, posing like the Burlington Northern Railroad goat himself, was a beautiful mountain billy about 35 yards away. I ascertained there'd be no getting any closer to this fellow, so I carefully drew my 55-pound recurve and shot. My bow-string struck the sleeve of my coat causing my arrow to strike the ground right in front of the goat. Now, I'm not kidding (pardon the pun), this goat bent its neck down and sniffed the arrow and then stepped on it. I could see it break right in half! He then turned and unhurriedly moseyed over the ridge.

I quickly headed in the direction he took. As I arrived at the spot where my severed arrow lay, I peered down and discovered that I was standing on slick frozen grass. Another problem cropped up. I began to slide down the sloping hillside. I tried to kick my boots into the grass for better footing, but I continued to slide precariously close to a drop-off. Faster I skied heading for the edge. At the last possible moment, I frantically grabbed a small fir tree and came to a jolting halt before going down the thousand foot drop. With fear and trepidation, I crawled back up the slope to safety.

That was the one and only shot I ever took at a goat. But it was by far not the last of my adventures with them. It wasn't until 1984 that I was lucky enough to be drawn again—or should I say unlucky enough. There is an area in the Olympic Mountains near my home that has a huge goat population. They freely travel from the national park and into the edges of the national forest. The goats are not indigenous to the park, they were introduced after the turn of the century. Since then, the park people have wanted them eradicated, because they are so destructive to the sensitive alpine environment.

Before and during the short hunting season, a large contingent of a so-called environmental group took it upon themselves to protect the goats from the inhumane bowhunters. With firecrackers and other noise makers, these benevolent saviors of all outdoors drove the goats safely into the national park. Only one of us 10 permit holders got a goat. I was not eligible to apply for the goat drawing for three more years, and I have been unsuccessful since. But, alas, my knee now has arthritis, and alpine traipsing is a thing of the past.

Yes, the goats were safe for another year, but the delicate environs of the park's timberlines would suffer more rigors from the goats' destructive eating habits.

The following summer, I took a boy scout troop on a hiking trip up to where I had been goat hunting the previous season. We made camp in a flat meadow on the side of a steep mountain. Just before dark, we started seeing a few goats around the camp. This thrilled the boys. It was such a stunning night, that I decided to sleep out in the open under the stars. Most of the boys chose tents. The other adult leader picked a spot next to a huge rock to lay his sleeping bag.

The camp was quiet as I laid on my back gazing up into the heavens. I started drifting off into blessed slumber. Do you know the feeling of being between two worlds just as you drift off to sleep? I was that way when I dreamed of a herd of buffalo stampeding through camp. The hooves got louder and louder, and suddenly I awoke, but it wasn't a dream. Under the bright moonlit sky, I could see the silvery forms of sheeny mountain goats springing everywhere throughout the camp like ghostly aberrations. One crashed into a tent rope, and the tent came down upon its occupants.

Then I heard, "Fred, one's got me cornered over here!" It was the other scout leader. In the moonlight 1 could see him standing in his underwear beside the big rock. A large goat was standing firmly a dozen feet in front of him. I quickly grabbed a slingshot I had near my pack and picked up a couple of rocks from the ground. The goat appeared ready to do some business with the scout leader. I raised the slingshot and shot a rock right into the side of the old goat. It turned and whirled away. Well, we eventually put camp back in order and tried to go back to sleep.

It seems that mountain goats crave salts. These goats had discovered that people urinate when camping. The urine salts evidently were highly prized on the goats' menu. They'd stalk a camp and then lick the urine deposits left by the campers.

As I lay in my sleeping bag, I heard soft footfalls again. Then right above my face appeared the ghostly head of a goat. It was more than I could take. I imagined what it would feel like to have a 250-pound goat place his paw on me. I reached up and slapped it away. The camp was invaded again. I grabbed a small transistor radio and turned on some loud music, but the goats seem to enjoy it. They rocked and rolled around us the rest of the night.

At the break of dawn, several red-eyed scouts and two leaders decided to descend from the goats' craggy playground and try their luck at trout fishing in the valley below.

Wilhelm brothers in their special 1930's hunting car.

Chapter 18
OH! THE ADVENTURE OF IT ALL

When we discuss traditional hunting archery, we have to examine the concept of adventure. I say this because I have been acquainted with hunters all of my life, and a thread of adventure runs through them all. When an archer picks up his bow and quiver and sets forth to the game field, there is a desire for adventure in his heart. The dictionary defines "adventure" as: an undertaking involving danger and unknown risks; a remarkable experience; the encountering of risks; to expose to danger or loss; to take a risk; to try; and to proceed despite danger and risk. Most of us hunting archers don't usually say when we go hunting, "I'm going out to expose myself to danger and risk." Quite the contrary—but, deep inside us is that desire to come across the unexpected, challenge it, and then conquer it. If this is not in our hearts, then we usually quit the sport. Yes, which one of us has not relished coming home the victor after meeting up with a fine and unexpected adventure?

Challenge is the operative word in traditional bowhunting. Personal basic human input is the challenge that drives us to adventure. Take away the personal human element, then the desire is lost, and the adventure turns meaningless. In our high-tech society, we are bombarded with new technology that diminishes human input.

Quite often our adventures start as questions such as: "Can I go into that field, find and stalk within 20 yards of a whitetail buck; if I can, do I have enough mental and physical skills to kill him with my bow and arrow; and do I have the knowledge and ability to dress, skin, and butcher the deer correctly?" When these questions have been proposed, either consciously or not, we then work on their solutions. We practice stalking and shooting and read about cleaning and butchering. Remember that challenge is the human input. We may also ask: "Can I stalk within shooting range without too much technology such as artificial scents and camo clothing; and can I shoot the animal using my own power and instincts rather than relying on highly refined aiming and shooting devices?" When we find solutions to our questions, we discover that it is the whole process that brings us satisfaction—not just the kill.

Adventure is the act—not the end product. Some people get confused here. Adventuring, for example, is the act of climbing the mountain—not just reaching the top; it is the act of hunting—not just killing. Arriving at the summit is the climber's goal, and it's important; bagging the game is the hunter's goal, and it's somewhat important. But it is the total process of adventuring that compels us to do what we do.

Adventure is often synonymous with travel. Travel to any game field will do for the experience of adventure. Any wild area will suffice, not exclusively far away places with strange sounding names. I am acquainted with a fellow that is blessed with considerable money. He buys all of the finest equipment. He travels to exotic, far-off game fields around the world and hires professional guides to place him on the best hunting stands. The guides do most of the work, my acquaintance does the killing. He has a grand old time and is somewhat puffed-up with his exotic trophies.

I know another man that grubs out a modest living. He is busy raising a bunch of kids. He makes most all of his equipment. He hunts the hills near his home and has to study hard to find animals. The game in his area is usually heavily hunted, therefore, he has had to develop outstanding stalking skills. Regardless, he regularly fills his tag. This fellow loves to tell of his exploits and adventures, but seldom does he brag.

I ask you, which fellow is having a greater adventure? Whatever your answer is, I believe you can see that true adventure can be found most anywhere—so long as there is a challenge to it.

Adventure has no respect for age, sex, or race. Anyone may participate. Unexpected trials or events can come to all, and they are the spice of adventuring. Quite often, this seasoning is unwanted. Indeed, most hunters make careful preparation to avoid it. Sometimes these unexpected events may even cause death. Fool-hardy adventurers do not last. They run into too many unplanned trials.

About ten years ago, I had quite an unexpected adventure. I drove over to one of my favorite hunting areas in the Cascade Mountains. It was early in October, and the mountains were spectacularly adorned in their fall raiment. The warm morning sun was invigorating. As I grabbed my longbow and quiver, I entered a mental debate over the pros and cons of carrying a heavy jacket on my sojourn. "It's too nice to pack that heavy thing," I decided, and took a light windbreaker in its place and a small emergency kit.

I noticed that a new logging road had been cut back into the mountain, and it started near where I normally park my car. I headed west from the new road on a wilderness trail that would snake its way four or five miles up the mountain. I was very well acquainted with this trail. A fine morning it was, and I spotted several deer, but I took no shots. I feel sorry for flatlanders who never get the opportunity to hunt the western mountains in such splendid conditions.

Later, towards early afternoon, my fortune started to sour. I came across a new logging road and assumed it was the same one that came out near where I had parked. The weather was changing, too. Heavy, dark clouds were rapidly filling the sky, and the temperature was dropping. I turned left on the new road, and decided that it would be best to travel straight to my car instead of following my tracks back down the wilderness trail. I walked that dirt road for over an hour, when I realized that it wasn't heading to where I thought. I kept on that road for half an hour more and was getting wet from a sudden rainstorm. I plodded on. "Fred," I said, "you have gotten yourself into a survival type situation, and you better build yourself a shelter before it gets too dark."

A few hundred yards further down the road, I spotted a light glowing in a clearing. "Great!" I thought. "I'll just go over there and get someone to drive me to my car." It was dark when I got near the camplight. The camp was about a hundred yards off the road, and I couldn't see a way over to it, so I yelled, "Hey, in camp! I'm lost and need a ride to the Julius trailhead!" Even from that distance, I could hear the distinct metallic sound of a cartridge being jacked into a chamber. I yelled out again. This time a reply came back from a couple of guys calling me all sorts of foul names, and telling me in no uncertain words where to go and what would happen if I approached their camp. (I found out later that they had a marijuana-growing operation going.)

Remembering a very large brush pile I had seen back up the road, I went to it and started arranging a bonfire. I took out my emergency kit, thankful for having had the sense to bring it along. Then I saw them, high up on the mountain, lights dancing down the road—no bigger than specks. Next, I heard them—motorcycles! My grief was transformed into joy, as they came. It turned out to be four guys on three-wheeled A.T.V.'s and I hailed them to a stop. More than happy to help me out of my plight, one fellow told me to hop up behind him. Now, I never really liked these three-wheelers but was more than happy to ride on one then.

Off we went down the muddy road, with me holding on for dear life, certain I was going to die. These guys where really high-balling it. My driver turned his head back toward me and said something. It was then that I detected the stench of alcohol on his breath. Now I was positive I was in the Grim Reaper's grasp. But after a harrowing five-mile ride, we rattled up to my car. By then it was snowing heavily, and I was shaking from the cold—a sure sign that hypothermia was setting in. I bade my rescuers a fond farewell and changed into some dry clothes.

Snow was rapidly collecting on the road as I made the 25-mile drive to the top of the pass. I hadn't thought that tire chains would be necessary this early in the year, so I didn't pack them. I slipped and slid over the pass with my fingers pressing impressions into the steering wheel.

Late that night, when I got home my wife asked, "How was your trip?"

"Splendid!" I replied.

I had another unusual, unplanned adventure with my partner, Ron. We were chasing elk in the Olympic Mountains. The weather was clear, sunny, and cold, but night-time was bone freezing. Late one afternoon, we found some fresh elk tracks in the snow crossing a logging road. We followed the tracks a bit before they split off into two different directions. I followed one group and Ron took the other. After some lengthy tracking, I decided to go back to Ron's car before dark. When I reached the car, Ron wasn't back. I waited while winter darkness was quickly settling.

I thought it would be a good idea to follow Ron's track a ways in the increasing darkness, then I could yell in hopes that he would follow my voice to safety. Night enfolded the forest, and I shouted for Ron—no answer. I waited and hollered again. Then I heard his faint voice from across a canyon, telling me that he was stuck on a hillside and couldn't see. I yelled, asking him if he had a flashlight in the car. He replied no. I shouted back for him to stay put, while I went for some help. The nearest place was a state prison facility about five miles away. I could envision Ron sitting, freezing cold, on that dark, lonely mountain side with the temperature hovering around minus five degrees.

I drove up to the prison with the goal of having someone phone a sheriff's deputy. Now, here comes a real adventure. I walked up to the business door and pushed the button. I must have looked pretty strange standing in my hunting garb in the darkness of night. A voice came over a speaker telling me to state my business. I replied that I had a hunting partner stuck up in the hills, etc. The voice told me to stand still and wait. A full five minutes later, a uniformed officer bade me come in. I was given a real grilling and told to wait some more. After about ten minutes, I guess they decided I wasn't there to lead a prison breakout. Next, I was ushered into another room where I was grilled again. Finally, they called the sheriff, and I was escorted back to the car and told to drive to the parking lot entrance to wait for the deputy with my doors locked.

The deputy arrived half an hour later in a big four-wheel drive K-Blazer. I had to retell the story again as he drove us back up the road. The deputy was a real big, amiable fellow who was at least one hundred pounds overweight, and to top it off, he had a bad cold and was hacking and wheezing. We parked, and as we walked up to the place where Ron was last heard, it was evident that this deputy was probably in worse shape than Ron. I had no problem convincing him that I should take his big flashlight and seek Ron alone.

I hollered out to Ron, and he guided me to him by his voice. It was a good thing that he stayed put, because there were some steep canyons where he could have fallen. Ron came out very cold and thankful that we reached him when we did.

Both of us were plenty embarrassed by our lack of preparation. When a hunter starts chasing elk, something crazy happens, and he often looses good sense. This was one escapade that Ron and I learned much from, and hopefully, one that we won't repeat.

Another part of adventuring is having others along with you. Shared adventures bring close friendships. You can often tell a man's mettle by how he handles trials and challenges. Many of us get very picky about our hunting companions, because a lot of people don't take to adventure very well. Good hunting partners are as hard to come by as alligators in Alaska. We all have prerequisites in our consideration of hunting companions. Saxton Pope and Art Young are espoused as classic examples of hunting buddies. Pope gave us good advice when describing Young. He said that Young had a good, even nature, was uncomplaining when the going got rough, was game for adventure, and of a high moral character. These virtues rank high on my list. Over the years, I have hunted with all sorts of people, but the ones I enjoy being with the most exemplify these standards. One bowman told me it was easier selecting his wife than finding a good "hunt'n partner."

Experiencing adventure vicariously is another facet. I can recall many pleasant times sitting around a wilderness campfire, listening to and sharing adventures. When several bowmen gather, conversation often centers around their daring escapades. This is especially true when the companions are well-seasoned, venturesome veterans who are no strangers to the wilds. Literature often plays a strong role in kindling the fires of adventure, and many of us enjoy reading about the daring accounts of others.

Adventure is found in discovery and the challenge of doing something that few have ever done. One doesn't have to go to distant lands to have a most excellent challenge. There once was a man who hunted the arboreal forest near home with a life-long hunting partner. One day, the old partner up and dies. (This was a rude thing, because good partners are hard to find.) The following season, the grief-stricken man made a vow to kill a great buck with his departed partner's own arrow as a tribute. Low and behold, he accomplished the challenge, and a grand escapade it was.

Sometimes we go too far with our challenges and get downright foolish. For example, I know of a fellow who undertook the challenge of shooting deer in excess of 100 yards. He was able to kill a few deer, but you can imagine the number of wounded animals he inflicted with his nonsense. I read about another man who set up the challenge of shooting rhinoceros with longbow and arrow. Rhinos have been killed before with arrows, so it was nothing new. Rhinos are diminishing from the wilds to the point of extinction—so why kill them? He had devised an arrow of solid fiberglass shafting to get enough penetration to kill the beast. In order to achieve accuracy with such unruly arrows, he had to get within 30 yards of the pachyderm. This was his challenge. But, if he really wanted a spicy challenge, he should have tried it without a rifle backup. An analogy of this is the stranger who wants to go into the roughest bar in Montana and act like one of the local boys. But, if things get too rough, he'll have a couple of bodyguards along to bail him out.

A fellow bought a longbow from me awhile back and he wanted to see if he could get a brown bear with it, using arrows tipped with chipped obsidian points. He went to his remote hunting ground alone and waited in a ground blind to ambush the bruin. When the bear came into a small clearing, he shot it through the chest. He hunkered down with fear, as the 1200-pound bear charged around the clearing howling and growling.

My customer said that after half a minute or so, the bear fell over dead, and that those 30 seconds were the longest and most hair-raising 30 seconds of his life.

Adventure and romance dance together—romance being the emotional appeal of the experience. Traditional hunting archers have a passion for going into remote, wild areas without too much modern technology. Maurice Thompson, in *Witchery of Archery*, tells of his notion of going on an extended hunt into the remote regions of 19th century Florida with a native Indian bowman and living off the land in a primitive way. This adventure was conceived in pure romance. Real hunters like to plan and dream of their upcoming adventures in romantic ways—whether they admit it or not. On cold winter days, I sit in my den and dream of stalking carp along a remote creek in the hot desert of central Washington. In my dream, I have my bow in hand and am attired in the barest of essentials.

Now, reader, you may think that carp shooting is not fraught with much danger and adventure, but not so. Beside the risk of falling in the water and drowning, there is also the risk of shooting yourself. As any well-seasoned carp slayer will attest, the risk of self-inflicted wounds is no laughing matter. The first time I witnessed this phenomenon was when I took a shot at a carp on the surface of a creek. I was standing on the bank, and the fish was a good 30 feet away. As the arrow sped to its target, a coil of line was under my foot. The heavy fiberglass fish-arrow came to an abrupt halt just before striking the fish. The taut line boomeranged the shaft straight back at me at a terrifying speed. There was nothing I could do but watch as it approached. Luckily, it missed by mere inches. To prevent similar occurrences, many avid fish shooters use a lighter line attached to the arrow— so that it breaks instead of boomeranging.

Some have not been so lucky. Just the other day, right here in the Northwest, a fellow shot at a carp. The line fowled and snapped the arrow back at him. The deadly shaft struck the poor guy in the eye piercing through his skull and into the brain, killing him.

One friend of mine hunts with a homemade, self-wood longbow, because he says it's romantic, and its simplicity makes his outing personally meaningful. I feel the same way about traditional clothing. I enjoy using my leather hunting shirt and moccasins in the wilds, even though they may not be as practical as other clothing. I guess I shun camo clothing because it is not romantic to me. Rambo clothing and longbows don't mix well in my fantasy.

Automobiles don't mix well either, but they are a necessity to provide transportation to the game field. Even the most staunch of the primitive equipment archers have forsaken foot power and the horse to get to where the game lives. In planning a romantic adventure afield, the car is left parked somewhere, and the hunting is done on foot, horseback, or maybe canoe from there. Road hunting in an auto lessens the romance.

On a good share of my outings, I come home empty handed as far as game is concerned. But I also come home with a storehouse of memories, experiences, and adventures that continue to live with me and enrich my soul.

Desert Bowman Tournament. Barstow, California, May 1949.

Section IV

PROFILES FROM THE DUST

THE GOLDEN CHAIN

When I was fifteen, I obtained a copy of *Witchery of Archery*. I read it practically from cover to cover in one sitting. Oh, the romance of this little book touched my soul! Here were two brothers, Maurice (the author) and Will Thompson, right after the Civil War, engaged in adventuring with the bow and arrow. They went into the swamps and fields and hunted everything. My philosophy exactly! At fifteen, I believed that every wild critter was fair game, too. What I didn't know then, but know now, is that their book has had its effect on thousands of people the same as it had on me.

The word "tradition" connotes history. So, when we refer to traditional archery, we basically mean archery with a long history. Of course, people are the main part of history. In this section, I would like to discuss some historical American bowmen that have played a meaningful role in our sport. I don't profess to cover a complete list, but I'll use my creative license to arbitrarily select a few that are significant.

Wherever congregations of traditional archers meet, there is always conversation about some historical bowmen—Howard Hill did this, or Art Young did that, etc. We seem to have a fascination with it. Often, because of our preoccupation, we ascribe new images to these people, and they become legendary. With such a rich history, including many people with legendary status, traditional archery is steeped with customs and myths.

When one goes into the field to shoot the time-honored bow and arrow, he goes with an inheritance that has come down from the dawn of mankind. He goes enriched with a kinship of earlier bowmen that once plied their skills as he does now. This golden chain weaves and connects him with them and justifies him and gives meaning to his sport. Therefore, it is of some value for archers to be acquainted with those earlier bowmen who have passed beyond the veil. In order to understand ourselves now, there is wisdom in learning about our predecessors.

William 'Chief' Compton (third from left)

Chapter 19
PROFILES

WILL COMPTON
"The Chief"

The person who was mostly responsible for introducing archery on the West Coast is little known. William John "Chief" Compton did for the West Coast what the Thompson brothers did for the East. Compton may have accomplished more, however, because he enthusiastically implanted in his many archery converts and students a love for hunting with bow and arrow. He was a great personal salesman for the sport. He lacks notoriety today because he didn't write a book, but in his day, he was the recognized leader in West Coast archery circles.

He was born during the Civil War, in 1863, in Flint, Michigan. He moved with his family to Nebraska at age seven. He loved being with the Sioux Indians. They adopted him and taught him their hunting and outdoor skills. They bestowed upon him the accolade of "Chief," and he proudly carried the name through life. Some people think archery in America came directly from the English. However, because of Compton's upbringing with the Sioux Indians, he brought this knowledge into our present day heritage.

He moved to Medford, Oregon, in 1883, and relocated to California around 1900, residing there until his death in 1938. While in California, he introduced the bow into the lives of many people. Among the Chief's most ardent pupils were Dr. Saxton Pope and Arthur Young. He brought them together and instilled in them a love for archery. He affected Pope so strongly that the doctor wrote *Hunting with the Bow-and-Arrow*. This book had an extensive effect, and the popularity of field archery spread across the West Coast.

The Chief was a commanding and colorful person. He looked a lot like a Sioux Indian himself and spoke with a rich voice.

His hunting ability was tremendous. He killed his first deer at age 14. Following that, numerous deer, elk, moose, and a buffalo were taken Indian style with the primitive bow. Pope claims that Compton could kill running small game and birds on the wing. At long distance game-shooting, he was especially accurate. The hunting prowess of Pope and Young overshadows Compton, but Pope concedes in his writings that the Chief was a better hunting shot than either he or Young.

The highest award of the National Field Archery Association given in recognition of outstanding contributions to archery (which is given sparingly) was initiated in 1947 and named for "Chief" Compton, one of the finest men in the history of our sport.

Art Young demonstrates his broadhead points on a lion bone.

ART YOUNG
"The Archer Adventurer"

A good share of archers know of Art Young. But they are only acquainted with him from books, magazines, and awards, because he died before most were born. Art himself was born in 1883 in California.

While working on a San Francisco newspaper as a young man, he met "Chief" Compton at the Panama Pacific Exposition. Compton, always willing to proselyte and teach, showed him how to shoot the bow. Being athletic by nature, Young became good at target shooting and was California State Champion several times between 1913 and 1920, but he claimed he was not too serious about the target game.

Hunting with the bow became a passion with him after meeting Saxton Pope and Ishi, the Yahi Indian, at the University of California archery range.

He gained notoriety because of Pope's books and a nature movie called "Alaskan Adventure," which was seen by hundreds of thousands. In this film, Young shoots sheep, moose, and brown bear. With this notoriety, he lectured at sportsmen shows, theaters, and colleges.

Young lived at a time when equipment for hunting was mostly homemade. Because he set out to hunt large and dangerous beasts that modern man had not yet tackled with bow and arrow, he had to invent, design, and develop equipment that would efficiently accomplish his purposes. Can you imagine his challenge to develop a metal broadhead that would dispatch a giant Kodiak brown bear, or a bow that would hold up when being carried for hundreds of miles on the hot, African savannas? From his experiences, Young came to recognize that arrows killed large game more effectively than bullets. Because of his successes, state game departments around the country accepted his notions on the arrow's killing capabilities and allowed special bow and arrow hunting seasons.

Art Young was considered a fine sportsman and gentleman by those who knew him. He was a temperate person and didn't smoke, drink, or swear.

The archery world mourned in 1935, when Art died from a ruptured appendix.

Saxton Pope with a porcupine.

SAXTON POPE
"Ku Wi, The Medicine Man"

In the 1920's, the world of archery was smitten with a book written by Saxton Pope, a surgeon and medical instructor at the University of California. Titled *Hunting with the Bow-and-Arrow*, it tells of the adventurous pioneer archery activities of Pope and his friends hunting in the early 1900's. This romantic book sparked a resurgence of interest in the sport, which has lasted even until today.

One can get to understand Saxton Pope from his writings. He graduated with honors in medicine at the University of California. The book illustrates his scientific thinking as he applied himself to archery. This is demonstrated in his discussions on how arrows kill, techniques for making equipment, and the study of primitive archery.

Americans were shocked in 1911 when an aboriginal Indian was found near Oroville, California. The nation thought that all of the native inhabitants had been conquered, but a last surveying member of the Yahi, a man about 60 years old, was captured on the outskirts of town. Eventually, he ended up living in the anthropological area of the University of California, where he became a world-wide celebrity. Ishi's beliefs prevented him from telling his personal name to anyone, so he was given the name Ishi, which means "man" in Yahi. It was at the university where Pope met Ishi. Being by nature a romantic, Pope befriended the Indian and set about learning the Yahi way of life. This kindled his interest in aboriginal archery. Under Ishi's tutelage, Pope hunted small game and deer.

"Chief" Compton introduced Pope to Art Young while Young practiced archery on the university range. A close friendship sprang up between the three—the "Chief" was the well-practiced, wise mentor; Art was the athlete with a gentle personality and adventurous heart; and Saxton was the organizer, wealthy, petulant and more high-strung. This trio took buffalo, grizzly bear, black bear, polar bear, brown bear, deer, moose, elk, African lions, plus other game.

In my opinion, the best and most exciting bow and arrow hunting story ever written was the account of Pope and Young hunting grizzlies in the middle of the night. This adventure can be found in Pope's book. The doctor also wrote an interesting book called *Adventurous Bowmen*. This was a diary-style book about Saxton's, Art's, and the renown author Stewart Edward White's escapades in East Africa shooting lions with the bow. According to Hugh Rich, Pope financed most of the safari.

Pope's writing style captures the fancies of the reader. When one reads Pope's essays, he cannot help but get a glimpse of pure traditional field archery. For example, he said in *The Adventurous Bowmen* that, "Man never had a more perfect weapon than a bow-and-arrow, from the standpoint of charm and intimate response. The bow becomes part of his mood; member of his faculties, yielding service and direct action in proportion to the throbbing life placed in it. The very sinews of the huntsmen are implicated in his weapon. The poise and nicety of his mental state is made manifest in the flight of his arrow. The serenity and steadfast nature of his nerves are registered in its true flight."

Pope died at the relatively young age of 51 (1875 - 1926) from pneumonia contracted while he was hunting in Africa. His legacy is too great to fully appreciate.

"The Legend"

HOWARD HILL
"Mr. Archery"

I never met Howard Hill. I wish I had; heaven knows he has meant a lot to me. As a teenager, I lived less than 200 miles from him in southern California. I regret not meeting him.

One evening in 1952, I saw a feature film called "Tembo," starring Howard Hill. He traveled from one adventure to another hunting all kinds of dangerous beasts with his faithful bow and arrow. What a terrific fellow! He had me so worked up that I took hard earned money and bought a new Ben Pearson archery set. From that time on, my life was changed. I didn't realize it then, but many other people had the same experience. In my opinion, no other person had such an impact on modern archery as Hill.

I really became involved in organized field archery soon after my start. Right away I began hearing disparaging remarks about Howard from lots of archers. Many claimed that he was a Hollywood phony. They pointed out how fake the movie "Tembo" was, giving examples of the leopard being chained while being shot, or that there was an Indian elephant used in the elephant shooting scenes, and on and on. In southern California, we had some very good shooters. They would offer Howard challenges to come and compete. Howard was seldom seen. This reinforced the idea that maybe he really was a fake. Even today there is a debate as to Howard Hill's abilities. I own a large number of his films (short subjects they called them at theaters) and boy, some of them are really corny—you cannot deny it! But, let's have a closer look.

Everyone agrees that Howard Hill was a very good athlete with considerable stature; remember that he was credited for shooting a 172-pound bow. I know that his shooting form was flawless. I know that he was a great advocate of practice. Sources have told me that he'd practice for four hours or more each day. With all of these factors, he certainly was a great shooter—not a fake. But, what about some obviously phony things we observe in his books and movies? There are the photos of him with his jaguar—look carefully—it's not a jaguar but a leopard! Now, why would he try to claim a leopard is a jaguar?

Hill started in the entertainment business in the 1930's. At the time, people attended lots of fairs, exhibitions, vaudeville, and movies for entertainment. During this period, anyone with unusual skills and a good stage presence could eke out a modest living. As with any business, promotion and advertising are important, and entertainers promoted themselves then as they do now. So Howard propagated himself as the "World's Greatest Archer" and traveled around doing his feats for crowds of people who loved the adventurous athlete-hero with the bow and arrow. Howard Hill reflected the entertainment and culture of his time (not ours). People were enamored of the stalwart cupid. His style and bravado is what carried him with his audiences and provided him with bread and bacon—an honorable profession—you bet!

Jealousy often rears its ugly head. It seems that people get great joy in bringing down others. Most of us have participated in this—woe unto us. I'm always dismayed at the way humans try to bring themselves up by slamming someone else down. I believe that a lot of Hill-bashing comes from jealous people.

Howard Hill was not the only archer participating in the entertainment trade. Several others were doing pretty much the same thing. Hugh Rich told me that a number of these "entertainment archers" were very good. But Howard was the only one to make a living out of shooting over a long period of time.

One great thing about Hill was his interest in young people. I have talked to many archers who received their start from him personally. Their stories are always the same. He was open and extremely encouraging. He never turned any youth away. He recognized his responsibility to be an honest example to young people. What greater thing can anyone do? I've known some great shooters who wouldn't give the time of day to young aspiring archers.

Many people have a misconception about Hill's shooting style. Bob Wesley, the very fine shooter from Mississippi, and a long time personal friend of Howard's, told me that Howard was always amazed that so many archers never really learn to properly shoot a bow and arrow. By this he meant that a proper archer should draw to a consistent anchor with good steady tension in the shoulders and back. And an aiming system should be used. Some people believe that Hill was a purely instinctive archer—but not so. He employed a split-vision aiming method. Because of this, he could shoot a set of six arrows into a good group. From my life-long research on Howard, I would advise anyone who would like to really get a feeling for Hill's shooting style to get ahold of Bob Wesley's book or video.

Traditional archery is flourishing today, for a large part, because of Howard Hill. The 1970's ushered in the compound, and traditional archery almost became extinct. Howard Hill Archery Co. out of Montana, and the bowmaker, John Schultz, were among the stalwarts that kept the Hill legend alive. They provided equipment and information for a small number of people who followed time-honored archery as practiced by Howard Hill. As for myself, I still capitalize on the Hill legend by marketing a Hill-style bow.

This brings me to another point of contention—the Hill-style bow. I am acquainted with more than a few who claim that Hill taught them personally how to make bows, and I believe them. There are some who claim that Hill developed his bows through them, and I ask just how many people was Hill in business with?

Hill liked to shoot heavy bows and shoot them often. He found that yew and osage were not durable and consistent enough for his purposes. He experimented around and came up with a tempered, split-bamboo bow. He also believed a bow should be long enough to eliminate finger pinch and straight-ended for stability. Therefore, his own bows were around 68 inches or so in length. Because they were laminated, he could build a backset or reflex into the limbs to help compensate for the self-bow limbs' tendency to take a natural set. Through most of the 1940's, Hill loved these bows. They did everything he wanted. They were dependable, rugged, consistent, accurate, and of good performance.

Hill became acquainted with a man from San Diego named Frank Eicholtz. Eicholtz was experimenting with various materials on composite bows and became the father of the modern composite bow. Like Hill, he felt that longer bows were the only way to go. But unlike Hill, Eicholtz felt that the recurve bow was much better.

One day Hill approached Eicholtz and asked him if fiberglass could be applied to one of his bows. Eicholtz told him to bring one down to his shop. He did, and Eicholtz backed and faced the bow with fiberglass. Hill was very impressed by the increased performance. From there, Eicholtz did more work for Hill. And thus the modern Howard Hill style was born. In 1952, I bought a longbow from Frank Eicholtz that was of the original Howard Hill style.

In 1986, I went to the Great Lakes Longbow Invitational in Marshall, Michigan, and met a gentleman named John Lee. John showed me a Hill-style bow he had made. I was dumbfounded. I hadn't seen one like it for years. John had used rare tempered tonkin cane for the core. The nodes of the bamboo were left on the back, and the bow was backed by a thin strip of glass that followed the nodes. The belly was glass-faced, also. Never had I seen before, nor have I since, such a sweet and smooth Hill-style bow. John evidently had done a lot of good research and had some very good insight.

Like all good archers anywhere, Hill recognized that the arrow is the key to good shooting. Hugh Rich, who made many arrows for Hill, told me that Hill was very fussy about them; to a point where Hugh had a hard time dealing with him. Frank Eicholtz told me about an incident with Hill that was amazing. At an archery shoot in California, Eicholtz witnessed an incredible feat. Hill put a cardboard box into a tree. Next, he went around and got an arrow or two from all the archers there (youths, ladies, and men), and then using his own bow, he shot all of the various arrows into the box—quite remarkable!

Walt Wilhelm said of Howard, "We were together often. Hill was a good shot and great tackle-maker. He was very fussy about the finish on his gear and went to much work to have a perfect varnish finish on all his gear. Hill was a good stalker. The guy would work just as hard stalking a coyote or badger as he would a grizzly bear."

Over the years, I have heard a controversy about Hill's friendship with Errol Flynn. In 1937, Hill did the archery work for the movie "Robin Hood." He became well acquainted with the roguish Australian star of the movies, Errol Flynn. A friendship sprang up between the two of them, and it lasted until Flynn's death. Flynn was a real controversial figure. He was known for his fast living and unbridled escapades. Flynn was a great person for adventure. Howard and Errol hit it off and went on many larks together. Hill taught Flynn how to shoot the bow-and-arrow, and soon he was a good shot. One of their first adventures was pheasant hunting at night. The game warden caught them, and Errol tricked Howard into paying his $75 fine. The two of them also spent much time together hunting and fishing on Flynn's yacht "The Sirroco."

Flynn had a very shaky background and was involved with foreign political intrigue. According to Flynn's biographer, Charles Higham, he was also a Nazi spy. In 1958, Flynn was enamored of the fascist Batista government in Cuba. He was aware of the potential problem with Fidel Castro. He conceived a plan to have a friend invite Castro on a bow and arrow hunting trip. Hill would be along. At some point during the hunt, Hill would shoot and kill Castro and claim it as a hunting accident. Bazaar? You bet! Flynn never told Hill of his fantastic, savage scheme.

Howard Hill was an athletic, adventurous, handsome man. Errol Flynn looked up to him. They looked remarkably similar except that Howard was a few inches taller and heavier. Unlike Flynn, Hill was a God-fearing man who was totally faithful to his wife. People asked Hill how could he hang around with Flynn and his Hollywood gang and go unscathed. He answered that he went with them and observed but didn't feel the need to participate.

As I knock around in archery, I find that most everyone has a Howard Hill story—especially us older goats. A lot of these tales take on a Paul Bunyan quality. There is one that strikes my fancy. I have heard it from various sources—some claiming they heard it form Howard's lips. Howard Hill loved to play jokes and have fun. Being that he had a likable out-going personality, people generally enjoyed being around him and his pranks. It seems that the great archery manufacturer, Fred Bear, was not always taken by Hill's antics, however, and their personal relationship was sometimes strained.

As the story goes, Hill, Fred Bear, and others were participating in some kind of national hunting contest in Wyoming. The rules stated that in order to win the contest, each archer was allowed only one arrow to be shot only once at a pronghorn antelope. Hill took his shot from a blind, and his bow tip struck the blind, ruining the shot. He went back to the contest headquarters and notified the officials that he was eliminated. He then took a quiver full of arrows and went back hunting just to fill his tag. Hill had noticed, in his travels, that there was a number of pronghorn around Fred Bear's blind. So he proceeded in his jeep to an area close to Bear's. As luck would have it, Hill killed a pronghorn. He thought it would be great fun to drive over to Bear's blind and show off to him. What Hill didn't know was that Bear was trying to get two antelope to line up just right in order to shoot two animals with one arrow. Bear had patiently been waiting all that time for the perfect moment. Finally, Bear had two pronghorns standing in the correct positions. He was just starting to draw his arrow, when a grinning Hill came bopping up in his jeep. The antelope scattered, and an enraged Fred Bear went charging over to Hill, fully intending to physically modify his grin. When Hill saw the outraged Bear, he knew he had done something foolish and tried to shamefully apologize. Bear started to come after Hill but thought better of it when Hill put his big hands on his shoulders and told him to settle down. Hill admitted in later years that he was totally wrong. Fred Bear steamed about the episode afterwards for sometime.

Everyone who loves hunting with the bow and arrow ought to read Hill's book *Hunting the Hard Way* This book pretty much spells out Hill's philosophies and shooting style. Craig Ekin wrote a good biography of Howard called *Howard Hill the Man and the Legend*. Both of these books are available if you look for them.

I have heard a number of Hill's contemporaries talk about him. These are people who knew him. Some called him a clown; some have elevated him to a saint. I suppose, like all of us, he is somewhere in between. But I remember reading of his adventures in my youth and being thrilled. If there is a special place in the Great Beyond where all good archers go to discuss and relive the earthly sylvan experiences with bow and quiver, I hope to be there and look up Howard and shake his hand and say, "Thanks, for giving me a lifetime of enjoyment, my friend."

Walt Wilhelm gets a bear.

KEN AND WALT WILHELM
"The Brothers"

When I really started getting involved in organized field archery, around 1954, I began hearing about a group of archers that would meet up in the California desert country for fun shoots. They included: Earl Stanley Gardner, the author of the Perry Mason books; Nubbie Pate, a one-legged archer; Osage Jim Murphy, a locally renown archer; Howard Hill; Roy Hodde; John Laufler; Joe Golden; Jack Willard; Bob Morley; Bill Otto; Curtis and Ed Hill; George Brommers; Willard Bacon; and a host of other fine shooters including Ken and Walt Wilhelm. As time passed, I heard more and more about these boys—especially the Wilhelms. Unfortunately for me, their generation was passing as mine was beginning. I did, however, start collecting information about them, and from my research I believe that the activities of these men epitomize the true meaning of traditional archery. Two of these fellows stand at the forefront, Ken and Walt Wilhelm.

In 1908, when Walt was about seven years old, he lived in Idaho among the Blackfoot Indians. His parents later moved to northern Nevada where he and his brothers and sister were raised among the Paiute and Shoshone Indians. The boys were interested in the Indian lifestyle the rest of their lives, but it wasn't until the early 1920's that Walt became interested in bows and arrows as a sport. The more he shot, the more he loved archery. Walt and Ken eventually settled in the desert country near Yermo, California, and they became very active in archery. They met a number of prominent West Coast archers including "Chief" Compton. Because they all had Indian backgrounds, they became friends.

Ken and Walt went all over the country looking for wood to make bows. They cut yew, osage, palma brava, hickory, mesquite, and other varieties. They thought that juniper made some of their best bows, and they went all the way to Mt. Charleston,

Nevada, to the traditional Indian cutting grounds to get theirs. The two found that placing the green wood staves in the hot desert sand was the best way to cure bow wood—especially osage orange. They would take cedar and redwood railroad ties and split out arrow billets and plane them into shafts. Both preferred using wild bird feathers for fletching. Eagle, hawk, and crow were their favorites. "Just seemed like wild things fitted the game better," Walt said. Walt was good at working metal, and he made his broadheads from old cross-cut saw blades.

Archers started dropping by the desert to shoot with Ken and Walt. Soon, numerous fellows were coming to participate. They'd shoot at everything for fun. They had target ranges set up and unlimited small game to hunt. This group especially enjoyed crossing the desert in an old jalopy and taking adventure as it came. To improve their hunting skills, they'd tie a ham in a tree and then shoot it to check for arrow penetration. "They were a great gang of sportsmen in those days," said Walt. "One time, while hunting in the woods near my home, a gang of us had been shooting at a wildcat on the run. We'd all had a shot or two and missed. Then we got the cat cornered in a mesquite thicket. We'd all busted some arrows on close misses. After a lot of shooting and yelling, the old cat climbed out on a limb in plain view. We all stood and looked; there were about six of us. Ed Hill said, 'Listen, you guys, we've all had a lot of fun with this cat, so why don't we just let him go?' And that is what we did. I shot a few pictures, and we went looking for another cat!"

During the 1930's, Ken Wilhelm took a hankering for flight shooting. Ken was a small man but very tough and strong. Hugh Rich said that shaking this gentle person's hand was like putting your hand in a vise. Flight shooters should be strong. Ken could shoot a 125-pound, 4'6", osage bow bare fingered over 550 yards! He traveled around the country going to flight events, and his best footbow record was a world record 896 yards shot in Amarillo, Texas, in August, 1939.

Ken had another special talent. He was deadly accurate throwing golf ball size rocks. He would have someone throw a pop can high in the air, and then he'd quickly pitch a rock at it and knock it out of the air. He seldom missed. Even when he was in his seventies, he could accurately perform this stunt. Walt said that in 1924, Ken was a baseball pitcher for the southern California Vernon Club. In an exhibition game, Ken threw 15 balls to the legendary Babe Ruth and struck him out five times! Ken was asked why he was not pitching in the Major Leagues. In his typical, mild-mannered way Ken answered, "I like to be home with my family."

Ken also taught many to shoot the bow and arrow. Cowboy actor Roy Rogers was one of his students.

By the 1930's, Walt was writing archery stories and getting some notoriety. The motion picture industry was looking for novel ways to entertain their audiences. Ken and Walt, with their down-to-earth, home-spun ways, were naturals. They starred in four short-subject films for Paramount Pictures. These were "Death Valley Thrills," "Like Father, Like Son," "A Desert Adventure," and "Meet the Champs." Later, both made many radio and T.V. appearances including Art Baker's "You Asked for It." During the late 1930's, Ken and Walt were doing archery exhibitions and trick shooting. This went on until 1954. They performed in practically every major U.S. and Canadian city and even Europe.

In exhibitions and films, the Wilhelms performed some out-standing tricks. One that sends chills down my back every time I view it, is from their 1938 film "A Desert Adventure." It has Ken shooting a biscuit out of Walt's mouth. Another had Ken shooting a sugar cube off Walt's ear. Walt was no slouch at trick shooting either, and he had an unusual anchor—he drew to his hip. This was because he had severely broken his shoulder when he was younger. The great old flight shooter, Davy Davis, said Walt could have outshot everybody if he wasn't hampered with this disability. Both brothers were snap shooters. Ken could shoot left-handed as well as right-handed. In some of the boys' more spectacular acts, Ken shot either a collar button or a dime off Walt's head at 30 feet. Ken would hold a match, and Walt would light it at the same distance. They never had one accident in their years of performing.

Once, the brothers used their talent to rescue stranded flood victims along the Mojave River. Using arrows attached to lines,

Ken Wilhelm shooting world record 846 yards in 1938.

*Scene from their movie, Ken shooting a biscuit
out of Walt's mouth. Gus, don't try this!*

they aimed toward the roof of a house being carried downstream. The lines formed a lifeline, enabling the people perched on top the house to be rescued.

One of the best hunting stories I've ever heard was about the time Ken and Walt went to Mono County in California to look for the "Lost Mexican Mine" in about 1932. They made camp at a place called Leavitt Meadows, which was about 8,000 feet in elevation. Walt called it "God's Country." The boys spent a few weeks or so in late September and early October exploring and hunting. They killed a deer for camp meat and a rather unruly black bear that was robbing the camp while they were on their mining expeditions. During one of their mining jaunts, they happened across a magnificent buck deer late one afternoon. Being that they didn't have the bows with them, they decided to go out the next morning and hunt him.

The day dawned bitterly windy and cold. The boys put on two pairs of Levis and all the shirts they had and stuffed jerky and cheese into their pockets. They took six arrows, wrapped canvas around the broadheads, and shoved them down the backs of their pants.

Ken was using a 70-pound, silk backed, yew flat bow made by Fred Bear. Walt had a very short, wide, sinew backed, 65-pound osage bow made by Ben Pearson. Ken called his bow "Rib-splitter," and Walt named his "Hells - Bells."

They proceeded around the timbered hills looking for the big buck, the wind and snow driving into their faces. They trudged up a long ridge with Ken in front. Near the top, Ken dropped to the snow and frantically motioned for Walt to lay flat, because there was something over the ridge.

When Walt peeked over the ridge he saw a huge, tom mountain lion 30 yards in front. The large cat had a porcupine cornered under a ledge and was trying to dislodge it. The lion had its back to Ken and Walt, and with the wind blowing so hard, it was totally preoccupied.

The boys had hunted together often enough that they didn't have to say a word to draw and release. They quickly rose and drew their bows in unison. The rear end of a mountain lion at

30 to 35 yards isn't a very large target. They shot simultaneously through the wind and snow. Ken's arrow hit behind the ribs, and Walt's struck just forward of the left hip. The cat turned and snapped at the arrows and rolled down a gully and into the brush. They threw their arms around each other in congratulations.

The lion was nine feet stretched out and in beautiful, prime condition. Because of the terrible weather, they couldn't skin him out. On the third day the storm let up but when they returned to get the cat, a couple of other mountain lions had gotten ahold of their trophy and cannibalized it.

I wrote earlier that the activities of these desert shooters epitomized traditional archery. This is why. These men enjoyed getting together and having good clean fun. They didn't take themselves too seriously. They worked hard and learned their sport. Making their own tackle was a major activity. The more natural their materials the better it was. Most all of these shooters said, in their elderly years, that the most important part of archery was not the great shooting nor the game bagged nor the fine equipment acquired; the most important part was the friendships made and cherished.

Hugh Rich, a man who loved archery with all his soul.

HUGH RICH
"The Arrow Maker"

I used archery tackle made by Hugh Rich ever since I was a boy, but in 1983 a friendship sprang up between us. Hugh loved archery, bow-and-arrow-making, archers, and all the history that goes with them. I knew several of his archery friends, and he loved to reminisce with me about the "good old days." Our friendship grew fairly close, even though we lived 1500 miles apart. I believe we hit it off because we were both archery romantics.

I include Hugh to my list of significant notables for several reasons: being a major archery supplier is one of them; being a founder of organizations such as Archery Manufacturers Organization and California Archers Hall of Fame is another; and finally, as a historian of the sport.

From the 1920's to the 1950's, archery was centered in California. This was the hub of the sport, even though it was popular elsewhere in the country. A lot of this was due to the mild climate where year-round participation was no problem, and excellent hunting abounded across the state. Hollywood served as a magnet to a few great shooters, and a blossoming outdoor sports-minded population supported dealers and manufacturers.

In the middle of all of this was Hugh Rich. Born in 1916, he began hunting with his father at the age of five. When he was 12, he rode a bicycle from Glendale to what is now the grounds of Magic Mountain amusement park and shot a deer with his .22 rifle. Hugh got started with the bow and arrow by age 11 at the Griffith Park archery range. At this early age, he learned how to fletch arrows using pins. Hugh was so good with it that he could fletch five dozen arrows an hour! Captain Jack Hoefer, a shop owner and notable archer, was very impressed with Hugh's abilities and gave him a job. At this tender age, Hugh

March 5, 1982

While hunting with Fred Bear,
Nibbie Pate, and Bob Morley near
Lander, Wyoming, I took this
antelope with a replaceable blade
broadhead—a first.

The signed and dated #100 bills
are my winnings for this lucky
event.

It gives me great pleasure to know
these things are in my friend
Glenn St. Charles's museum....

Hugh Reid

retrieved arrows and kept score for a number of great shooters such as Art Young and Saxton Pope.

As a young man, Hugh had a flair for business. By 1936, Captain Jack wanted to retire and offered to sell his shop to Hugh for $200. Hugh was $15 short of savings and had to take a loan from his father. A repayment schedule was worked out. Being that the shop and equipment was worth well over $2000, Hugh later suspicioned that his dad worked out a secret deal with Captain Jack and that was the reason he got the shop so cheaply.

Hugh built his archery business over the next few decades into a leading supplier of archery products. During this time, he met and worked with many famous people like Gary Cooper, William "Hopalong Cassidy" Boyd, Bing Crosby, Guy Madison, and a whole cast of other renowned characters. Hugh became acquainted with practically every famous bowman or archery dealer. His personal acquaintances read like "Who's Who in Archery."

Hugh was not a person who minced words. He was very forthright in his opinions. If a person was a fraud or phony, in any way, he'd let you know. I sure enjoyed talking to him about his dealings with people. He had a way of dispelling legends about some and making heroes out of others.

One thing I noticed right away about Hugh Rich was that he had a real sense of right and wrong, and he tried to do what was right. He showed genuine loyalty and love to his friends (which were many). His business dealings were honest. Back in 1947, he had some real crises. He had to move all of his outfit from Boise, Idaho, to Glendale, California. Almost broke, he told the owner of the truck rental that he was going to San Francisco, which was within the 500 miles rental limit. Anything over 500 miles would be an addition charge per mile, and Hugh didn't have the money. When the truck reached 500 miles, Hugh disconnected the mileage cable. The owner didn't suspect a thing. But old Hugh knew he had done wrong, and a couple of years later, when he was back on his feet, he gave the truck rental owner a personal check for what the original amount should have been. This fellow would tell this story to many others and laugh.

Hugh's first large order after becoming a shop owner was 100 lemonwood longbows for the University of Southern California. From there he made thousands more. But I believe what old Hugh did exceptionally well was the making of arrows. He could turn out high volumes of them and maintain quality. He understood correct arrow dynamics, also. Feather shape, nock alignment, point alignment, spine, weight, cresting, and finish were always top-notch. Howard Hill must have thought highly of Hugh's arrow prowess, too. When Hill was preparing for his African movie and archery safari, he was advertising for the Ben Pearson Co. He brought 10 gross (1440) of Pearson arrows over to Hugh to be checked for spine, straightness, nock alignment, and feather security. Hugh worked them all over and crest-coded them for grade. Other archers recognized the qualities of Hugh's arrows, because over 25 National Field Archery Association (N.F.A.A.) champs have used them.

Hugh was no slouch as a shooter either. From 1947 to 1949 he placed second in the N.F.A.A. bowhunter class championships, and he won first place in 1950. As a hunter, Hugh took much game. He was the first person to kill big game with replaceable bladed broadheads.

In his later years, Hugh was a little depressed with the transformation of archery. In his day, archery was held together by sportsmanship and camaraderie. Before he died, he related to me that the almighty dollar and commercialism had ruined the sport. But the resurgence of longbow shooters in the late 1980's had his spirits high again.

I remember a lengthy discussion with him about who was the best field archery shot in his recollection. We discussed Larry Hughs, Ande Vail, Howard Hill, "Doc" Pletcher, Ken Wilhelm and others. Hugh really thought Larry Hughs was right at the top. But he told me in colorful conclusion, "Fred, you take my words and try and move them any other way, other than Roy Dill and you're crazy. Roy Dill was the 1948 N.F.A.A. champion, when champion meant BEST!" Boy, I couldn't argue with Hugh on this one, because Roy Dill was a member of my archery club when I was a kid, and he really was a master with

Roy Dill tops Hugh Rich's list of best shooters.

Professional stage performing archers of the 1950's, Bob and Roy Dill, hamming it up.

bow and arrow. Both Roy Dill and his brother Bob did trick shooting for awhile. I remember seeing Bob's show when I was in junior high school. He shot the flame out from a lighted candle held in his wife's hand.

In our later conversations, Hugh confided about the grief he felt with the passing of his archery friends. Writing about his departed comrades was extremely difficult, but he felt obligated to put into written words the contributions made by his lifetime of acquaintanceship with archers. Hugh was a great letter writer and over the years he saved correspondence from his friends. He preserved other archery memorabilia. During his later years, he started compiling a history of modern traditional archery. This has helped many researchers find new perspective in the sport.

In 1990, after a lengthy illness, old Hugh went to join his chums at the eternal shoot.

Some claim that Ande Vail was the greatest trick shot–bar none!

ANDE VAIL
"Mr. Trick Shot"

Many contemporary archers believe that Howard Hill was the only person called on by Hollywood to do bow and arrow stunt shooting in movies—but not so. There were others. One of the best was a man named Ande Vail. He was born in 1920 and raised in southern California—in fact, he went to high school with Hugh Rich. He started shooting a bow at ten years of age, and by the time he was 16, he was making an income from archery.

Around 1938, Ande opened an archery shop in Glendale, California, on the corner of Ivy and Orange. Doug Easton was in an alley in Culver City, Henry Bitzenburger was using his father's lumberyard off Alameda in Los Angeles, Jack Hoefer was using an attic, and Hugh Rich had a single garage. But Ande Vail had a store front with a plate glass window.

From that time, Ande started doing trick shooting, and by the beginning of World War II, in 1942, he was known as "Mr. Trick Shot." The U.S.O. picked him up to do shows for the G.I.'s, and he did his perfected act at military bases around the world. He performed over 8,000 archery exhibitions, including trick shooting around a person—such as shooting apples off one's head and cigarettes out of one's mouth. His performances took him into the major movie studios to do stunt shooting in "Cowboy and Indian" films. Along with this, he did 21 short subject films on trick shooting and hunting. I still remember one of them with Ande hunting jaguars.

His other interests led him into research and medical work, and he became rather successful.

Ande died in 1985 in Boise, Idaho. Hugh Rich said of him, "I have known about every great archer in the last 50 years—Erwin Pletcher, Erwin Ketzler, Roy Dill, Frank Eicholtz, Willard Bacon, Larry Hughs, Poky Quail, Howard Hill, Rause Hinman, Bob Poppe, Dick Tone, Russ Reynolds, and many more fine gentlemen who would have considered it a privilege to have traded shots with Ande on a one-to-one basis." Then Hugh would slyly add, "When another famous shooter was winning his consecutive archery shoots, he would make sure that Ande Vail was not competing at them."

Roy Hoff's championship form in 1948.

ROY HOFF
"Mr. Archery Magazine"

Most archers today do not know of Roy Hoff. It seems that fame is fleeting. You see, from the late 1940's through the mid-1960's, Hoff was probably the most recognizable person in the sport of field archery other than Howard Hill or Fred Bear. He wasn't a great hunter, and he wasn't a great shooter, either. He was, however, a good hunter and a darn good shooter. What Hoff did was to solidify and tie the sport into a well-organized activity. Most people will probably never realize the lasting contributions he made to the sport.

Roy Hoff got started in archery in 1937. By 1945, he captured the championship in the newly formed N.F.A.A. He was mainly instrumental in securing a ten day pre-season archery hunting season in California. But, what really set him apart was his journalistic ability.

In February of 1944, he published the first edition of "Archery Magazine." It was the first slick-paper magazine devoted only to archery. He ran the magazine until 1969.

When I was a kid, I couldn't wait for each monthly installment to come out. The format was relatively simple. There were generally two or three hunting stories; coverage of some notable field archery shoot; lists of scores shot at various tournaments; a section on tackle making; wild game cooking recipes; new product releases; reports from the N.F.A.A.; a classifieds section; and lots of contributions from people around the country.

It was a hands-on magazine. People could write most anything on the sport and get coverage. This unsophistication gave the magazine its charm. People felt that it was "their magazine." Hoff used this to ply his political agenda—that agenda was to make field archery a unified, legitimate sport led by the N.F.A.A. From its inception until around 1965, the magazine had a hold on the hearts of archers everywhere. Because of this, the sport stayed intact and very much focused—thanks to Roy.

"Archery Magazine's" driving force was people. It portrayed archers as a group of unique comrades who participated in the very finest of activities. It was a professional journal, if you will, of bow and arrow shooters. It seems to me, that in today's market, most magazines of any sort are driven by commercialism; not just minor commercialism to pay for expenses, but major commercialism to put money into everyone's pockets.

In Roy's magazine the writers were regular fellows. The hunting stories were generally "Me and Joe Goes Hunt'n." These adventures, by common fellows, were down to earth and interesting. I was talking to an editor of a bowhunting magazine a few years ago, and he rather proudly told me that his magazine did not have any "Me and Joe Goes Hunt'n" stories. I have also noticed that his writers write the same old commercially-based gobbledy gook edition after edition. But Roy allowed everyday hunting stories by everyday fellows. He even rewarded the best ones with prize money. And the stories were much more intriguing, too.

Manufacturers and dealers loved the magazine. They knew that their products would be treated fairly in print. After all, it was their advertisements that prompted a lot of people to buy the magazine in the first place. Recognizing this, Hoff didn't try to fleece the advertisers with expensive rates.

As with a lot of good things, Roy Hoff had a love for the magazine and put his heart into it. I suppose that we'll never see another publication about the sport based on this kind of dedication. But we can take comfort in the fact that because of one individual, our history has certainly been enriched.

Roy Hoff passed away in 1985 at the age of 82.

Frank Eicholtz (note 'bowlock' draw and first centershot, takedown bow).

FRANK EICHOLTZ
"The Father Of The Laminated Bow"

I rode the San Diego Transit bus all the way out Adams Avenue to the archery shop. I had to make one transfer to get there. Upon entering the shop, I could tell that this was an exciting place. Strange looking bows lined the racks, boxes of arrows were displayed everywhere, target faces and animal horns adorned the walls, and the fragrant odor of Port Orford cedar permeated the air. Several men were chatting about bows in an unintelligible lingo. A thin, small, middle-aged man stopped what he was doing and came over to me. In a friendly voice, he asked, "Is there anything I can do for you?"

Being a young teenager, I was really impressed with the marvelous store and intimidated, too. This was obviously a place where men gathered. "I want to know what kind of a bow you think I should buy," I replied. The man patiently inquired as to my needs and wants and suggested a bow. He treated me like I was a regular fellow and dignified my request. This was my first dealing with Frank Eicholtz (he told me he pronounced it "Eye Holtz"). I never dreamed then that in later years I would be making bows for him. For the next dozen years or so, our paths crossed many times. I must say that I have met few people who know archery as well, and no one who knew as much about bows and bow making.

Back in the middle 1930's, Frank happened to be at Griffith Park in Los Angeles. There he found some archers having a small shoot. Howard Hill was amongst them, being idolized. At a break, Frank asked Howard if he might try to draw his 120-pound bow. Glancing at his slender 130-pound frame, Howard grinned and said, "Sure, go ahead and try it." Frank had no trouble drawing the bow. This impressed Howard, and he handed Frank some arrows and invited him to shoot. Frank did fairly well. This was the beginning of Frank's devotion to archery and also his friendship with Howard Hill.

Frank must have had the most efficient muscle attachment, because he could pull very heavy bows with his slender body.

At one time he kept a 105-pound bow strung at his shop. When some big lumberjack of a fellow would come by inquiring about purchasing a heavy bow, Frank's eyes would sparkle, and he would hand the 105-pounder to the customer. More often than not, the big guy would struggle trying to get even an angle to the string. "Hey, how heavy is this bow?" the fellow would ask. Frank would then take the bow and easily pull it a few times, the last time holding it for about ten seconds.

"Gee, this bow doesn't seem heavy to me." Frank would say. The customer would look at this slight man pulling the bow and ask to try again. The results would be the same, and any of us observing would be in stitches.

Frank Eicholtz shows perfect 'in-line' form.

By the early 1940's, Frank had made lots of bows and had come to the conclusion that the composite bow, as exhibited by the Turks, was the best. So, he began to redevelop the composite bow using newer materials. He started laminating Lamicoid, a plastic sign material, to the face of the bow. This worked well, but he needed a good tensile material.

World War II had spawned a lot of new technologies and materials. One of them was a wonder material dubbed "fiberglas." San Diego had a leading company in fiberglass, called Narmco. (The company still exists under a new name.) They made woven fiberglass sheets called "Conolon." (Some of you might be acquainted with "Conolon" fishing rods.) Frank applied this fiberglass to the back of a couple of bows with Lamicoid plastic on the facings. Harry Drake took a 50-pound flight bow which Frank created using this new composite construction to a flight shoot. A typical flight shot was 490 yards or so with bows in excess of 100 pounds. Harry shot the 50-pound bow well over 600 yards, and archery was revolutionized!

Frank discovered, through experimentation, that the yew core didn't have the properties he desired. It didn't have the shear strength and wouldn't hold up to the heating process very well. After much experimentation, he settled on maple. It was cheap, plentiful, mechanically strong, stable, and it glued well—clearly a superior core wood.

By this time, Frank had started producing composite bows commercially, and they were setting the archery world on fire. Howard Hill was interested in Eicholtz's revolutionary new process, so he went to see him. Frank applied fiberglass to a couple of his bows, and Hill marveled at their speed and consistency. He taught Howard how to use glass, plastics, glues, and other materials and supplied him for years.

When Howard Hill's book *Hunting the Hard Way* was published, it wasn't accepted too well by a number of archers. One reason was Hill's portrayal of the recurve bow as being so inaccurate for hunting—this at a time when the recurve was enjoying immense popularity. Right after the book was published, I asked Frank about this. One of Frank's stock model bows was depicted in the book. Frank said that once Howard was in his shop and took a recurve out to his practice target. Howard started shooting from every possible position and even while walking. He kept all the arrows in the center of the target. Frank couldn't understand what Howard meant by saying he couldn't shoot a recurve well. Frank expressed to me his disappointment in the negative depiction of his bow in Howard's book. Nevertheless, Frank and Howard remained friends. They respected each others abilities and their friendship.

Business was brisk for Frank in the early 1950's. He was selling bows and materials everywhere. He went to a friend, George Gordon, who was making fiberglass signs, and asked him to make his backings and facings. Before long, they were selling glass all over the world. Frank became very ill with an infection. After several weeks, he returned to business. Frank believed that during his absence Gordon turned out a large amount of bad glass. Eicholtz was bitter about this the rest of his life.

Eicholtz met up with a man from Costa Mesa and started his glass business anew. Frank developed what was later to be called the "Microflite" fiberglass arrow shaft. His new partner was killed in an auto accident, and because the patents weren't properly secured, Frank lost this business also.

There was another invention that Frank came up with. It didn't set the archery world afire, but it is certainly noteworthy. It is a non-mechanical release aid called a "bowlock." Quite a few people use them, including a number of champions. The bowlock is held in the drawing hand and hooked over the bowstring. The N.F.A.A. ruled it as a legal release, because it is shot with the fingers and not mechanically. I have used the bowlock extensively and have killed a half-dozen deer while employing it.

Frank was a traditionalist and didn't succumb to the compound as a number of his cohorts did. In the 1970's, Frank came up the some exotic laminates for facings and backings, including boron and graphite. He started offering recurves with extra long "hooks" to compete with the compounds. Bad health plagued him a long time and in 1983 he passed away.

I remember one special afternoon with Frank. I was 16 years old and was at an empty field archery range. A car pulled in and Frank got out and came over to the practice butts where I was. We shot for awhile, and he asked if I'd care to shoot the course with him. I was happy and scared at the same time. Here was a nationally recognized archer and maker of the finest bows asking lowly me to shoot with him. I accepted his offer, and we proceeded to go through the course. I remember how this soft-spoken man mentored me around the range in a most kindly way. I admired the way he instinctively murdered each target and never bragged or boasted.

Did I know the father of the laminated bow and the most inventive bowyer of modern times? You bet I did, and his name was Frank Eicholtz!

Among his many innovations Frank was the first to;

    use plastics in a bow.

    use maple bow core.

    use fiberglass bow-facing.

    use fiberglass bow-backing

    use graphite facings and backings.

    make quality fiberglass arrow shafts.

    make a center shot take down bow handle.

    make a practical bowstring release called a "bowlock".

THE OLD BOWMAN

Rise up, old bowman, the morning sun is caressing your windows! Rise up as in the days of your youth. Your bow is in the corner, and the quiver is on its peg. The day is fresh, and the woods beckon for roving. Rise out of your bed!

Think back through the years. Remember that vigorous young lad? He needn't any prodding. On a meager breakfast, he would shoot all day. That's right, old bowman, hop to it, get out there. Your young shadow will greet you. Hey, forget about that chore undone, the stiffness in the knee, the unpaid bill, the letter you have to write.

That's right, smell the clean breeze. Doesn't that sun brighten your spirit? Look! There is your shadow, your friend of a lifetime. Look at the joy in his step! Grab an arrow and pull the cord. Oh my, why haven't you done this more lately?

Watch that arrow wing up to the target. Try it again. Oh, what a wonderful shot, old bowman; you still remember! Do it again and again and again. I told you this is a marvelous day. Go here. Go there. Shoot here. Shoot there.

Your shadow is growing dim, old bowman. The sun's going down behind the trees. Night is coming on. Why so sad, old bowman? Might be awhile before you dance with your shadow again, eh? Going back to that undone chore, the stiff knee, the unpaid bill, the letter to write?

Put the quiver on its peg; hang the bow in the corner. Turn back the covers and sleep. Dream, old bowman. Dream of that shadow. He'll be waiting on the morrow. Dream, old bowman, dream.

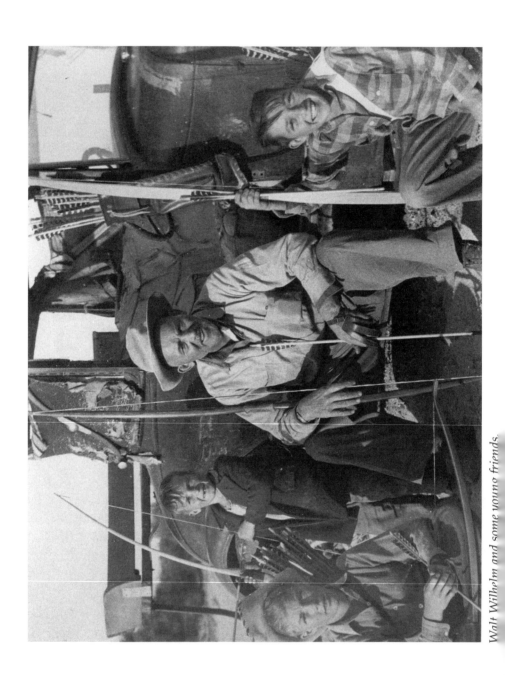

Walt Wilhelm and some young friends.

Section V

PHILOSOPHY

My teenage chum, Jack Wilson takes aim at a dove.

The author in 1953 with his Eicholtz longbow.

Chapter 20
TEEN TIMES

The house was quiet. A fire crackled in the wood stove. I was alone for the evening. I walked over to the bookshelf, took down an old picture album and returned to my chair next to the fire. Thumbing through the pages, a picture of Jack caught my attention. "Hi, Jack. Where have you been, and what have you been doing these last 30-odd years or so? Gads, has it really been that long since I've seen you?" Isn't life odd? I didn't even know where he lived or even if he was alive. After I had married, our lives went in different directions. I nostalgically looked at his picture. Those were the days—days consumed with hunting and fishing. I closed my eyes and mused sentimentally of my teen times.

Scenes were conjured in my mind's eye. Jack's Plymouth stopped in front of my folks' house. He walked in the back door. "You ready?" he asked, as his eyes glanced around the equipment on the floor. We were both around 17 years of age and were close friends since before grade school.

We began carrying the stuff out to the car. My mother watched us with the worried look that only a mother can have for a teenage son. "Don't worry, Mom, we're just going huntin' for a few days. We'll be okay." Not really convinced, she told us to be careful.

San Diego County, in the early 1950's, was an excellent place to hunt small game with a bow and arrow. Jack and I were in love with archery, and we had scouted the whole county for top-notch places. His car was loaded down with enough supplies to take us through an African safari. We had four or five bows, two or three hundred arrows of various styles and condition, food, clothing, and camping gear.

Our bows were recurves and straight-end composites. We had self-wood bows too. These we called longbows. Some of our bows we had made ourselves and some were bought. We made our arrows by the hundreds in Jack's den. Of course, we always carried an odd mixture of arrows that we found on local archery ranges. We used flu-flus, too, mainly to shoot at each other. (I did say we were teenagers.)

Our first stop was about twenty minutes out of town. This was a great place to warm up. There was a grassy slope below a ridge. We stood on the ridge and shot our arrows into the grassy slope at about a 60-yard range. We saw several doves coming and going in some nearby olive trees, and we went over and shot a few for our supper.

The next stop was up the coast a ways to a deserted beach. Here we used our poorest arrows shooting crabs off rocks. This sport wore old in a hurry, so we climbed a high cliff above the ocean and shot our broken arrows out to sea as far as we could cast them.

The day was slipping away as we launched ourselves into a special rabbit patch. Cottontails and jackrabbits were everywhere. In the early evening they would come out of hiding and make great sport for us. I had a supply of arrows tipped with Stemmler "Red Fox" broadheads and was anxious to see what effect they would have on a large jackrabbit. Walking down a ridge, I spied a jack sneaking up a gully in front of me. My 60-pound longbow laced an arrow through his stomach, and off he went. To us, a couple healthy lads, it was real sport chasing a wounded jack across acres of hillside trying to put in the killing shot. A half an hour later, we had him.

We had a favorite camping spot on a secluded bluff that was dotted with big old eucalyptus trees and overlooked a large lake. We would start a crackling fire and cook our camp meal. As twinkling stars appeared in the clear southern California sky, our sleeping bags were pulled near the fire. Weighty discussions would go late into the night concerning the philosophical matters of the teenage world.

The following morning we hastily ate, piled into the old car, and headed to a canyon that was a favorite resting place for vultures. In those days, vultures were fair game, and we wanted to get one. We located ourselves in a good spot and managed to get a few shots as they sailed over. The closest we came was to nip some wing tips.

Later that day, we were working down another canyon looking for adventure. Jack was above me, and I could hear him yell. Then a jackrabbit charged past me with an arrow sticking in its back. Jack was whooping right on its heels like a hounddog. I took up the chase, too. The rabbit was quickly outdistancing us, and just as he was about to disappear into some heavy brush, another arrow from Jack's bow caught him good and finished the race.

As we proceeded down the hill looking for more mischief, we came upon an old, rusted-out, abandoned automobile. We were about 130 yards uphill from it. "I bet you can't hit it from here," I was challenged. We were always challenging each other.

"That's too easy," I lied. "Bet I can put an arrow through the side front window before you can." I don't remember if either of us got one through the window or not, but we sure smacked that car several times. The day followed that routine of hunting a little and fooling around a lot.

The evening found us back at our camp. We always kept a campfire going. Our evening meal was cooked over the campfire in the most expedient fashion. We'd just toss a couple of cans of beans, stew, tamales, or some such in the coals. When the hot cans were opened, we'd eat directly from them with spoons. On the side, we would wash bread and donuts down with soda pop. This was really living. Often, you'd find us broiling a rabbit or some doves as a snack.

Two of our bows were always left strung at night in case of wolves, bears, mountain lions, or a sudden invasion of Martians. There was many a night we had close calls, but the morning always brought safety.

The last day of this hunt, we ended up road-hunting for ground squirrels. Now, the most low-down creature has to be a road-hunter, but our evil was rationalized by saying we were doing the farmers a favor. We would slowly drive down the back roads and look for squirrels perched up on their lookouts.

Then one of us would slip out of the car and try to put a feathered shaft through him. I made a dandy long shot on one that was camped on a high rock. Both Jack and I hooted gleefully. That is the great thing about a real hunting pal, he gets as excited about your successes as you do.

There were lots of squirrels in the area. We saw a farmer leaving his pasture and asked him for permission to hunt it. He gave a strange smile and told us to go ahead but be sure to close the gate and not to shoot any of the cattle. In the middle of the pasture was a rocky area, and we had some rare shooting on the little rodents. After awhile, the squirrel village was completely quiet, so we headed out across the pasture towards the car. "Hey, Jack, those are really friendly cows. Look, they're following us."

"Boy, that one cow is sure a big one!" Jack exclaimed as it started trotting towards us. The remembrance of the farmer's strange smile crossed my mind. It was then that we could see that our cows were really bulls. The race began. I never went through a fence so fast.

Jack and I had lots of great fun with our bows and arrows. There is something natural about boys and their affinity for archery. Yes, those were the years. I pushed another log into the stove, it was hard to stay in my reverie.

San Diego, California, where I was bread and buttered, has a huge park right in the middle of it. Balboa Park is one of the many charms of the city. The famous zoo is but a small part. A nine-hole and an 18-hole golf course lie within the park also. During the early 1950's, we lived a few blocks from the golf courses. As a young teenager, I naturally gravitated to the park and golf courses for fun and adventure.

A couple of hours before dark every evening, the courses were cleared of golfers, and the greens keepers would repair, water, and mow them. This was an ideal time for a youngster to go to the course and scour the edges for lost golf balls. These golf balls could be sold for pocket money. A major obstacle at the time was the German grounds keeper we called Fritz. He patrolled the courses in his open, surplus army jeep with fierce determination. Fritz would try to chase us down with the vehicle and hold us for the police. Fritz was a formidable, fearsome foe.

An amazing thing happened in those days as the shadows of evening etched across the fairway valleys. Rabbits by the hundreds would creep from the chaparral edges onto the grassy green course and start their evening meal. What a fantastic sight it was to a budding archer. With my little spaniel and trusty bow, I'd be waiting for the evening bunny migration. Cottontails and jackrabbits crowded into bunches like African game herds (this was my fantasy). Valley quail, doves, possum, and foxes also abounded. The trick for us, myself and my teenage archery pals, was to slip around and try to put an arrow into the rabbit herds without being discovered by Fritz and his evil jeep.

My best friend Jack Wilson and I were in a small-game hunter's paradise. One of our best stunts would be to go to one of the fairways on the hilltop. From there, we'd look for rabbit herds in a canyon fairway below. Sometimes a herd bunched up in a 20-foot diameter so closely packed, the grass under them couldn't be seen. We'd each take a field-tipped arrow from our quivers and cast a wary eye for Fritz. Next, we would take our best flight stance and simultaneously shoot our arrows high out over the hillside, down and out on the lower fairway toward the rabbit herd. Usually our first shots missed. The rabbits often would not notice. But now we had our trajectory figured out! Again our shafts were cast out and down, right into the herd. In one motion, the whole fleet of bunnies would charge off the grass into the brush. With luck, there would be an arrow sticking through a rabbit.

One fine southern California evening, we launched our arrows and impaled a big jack. It went running up the fairway with a shaft sticking out like a periscope. Around a dog-leg and out of sight it went. Now, the toughest animal to put down with an arrow is a big jackrabbit. To us boys, the real fun had just begun. We charged off in distant pursuit. When we got to the lower fairway, we turned and headed up the course in the direction we'd last seen the jack. All at once the rabbit was heading towards us. This was strange. Then we noticed what changed the rabbit's direction. Coming straight for us was Fritz! My friend, Jack, went in one direction, I in another, and the rabbit in still another. But, woe unto me. Fritz took my trail! I raced across the fairway heading for a large patch of scrub-brush and chaparral. Quiver and arrows were bouncing and dancing all around as I zipped for protection like some harried rabbit myself. I could hear Fritz's jeep chugging right on my heels as I entered the safety of the brush. Then the air thundered with German words that I could not understand but knew the meaning perfectly well. From a distance I yelled back, "Fritz, you'll never catch me—you bow legged jackass!" I could see him by his jeep hopping up and down and frantically shaking his fist at me.

"Ya, I get you, bad boy. When I do, you be very sorry!" He boomed back. Later, Jack and I would rendezvous and savor our adventure.

One evening, as I sneaked across a fairway in pursuit of a bunny, I heard a strange hissing sound. I stopped to listen, then all around me a myriad of water sprinklers suddenly jolted to life, and I heard a deep German voice in the distance happily proclaiming victory.

I was very fussy about my arrows in those days. The main quality I insisted upon was that they had to be cheap!!! If they weren't cheap they were no good. My reasons were these: First of all, I didn't have a lot of money; and secondly, I loved to shoot lots of arrows and take reckless shots and I didn't want to spend much time looking for lost, expensive arrows. A typical arrow from my quiver would be made from lacquer-covered cedar. It would have three fletch, five and one-half inch, grey bar feathers and cheap plastic nocks. The points would be old .38 casings or field heads. I would generally make these arrows in the hundred lot.

I supported my arrow habit by mowing lawns, finding lost golf balls, and other odds-and-ends jobs. I generally made about 75 cents an hour. I hated the hard work then, but as I look back on it, I realize it taught me how to work—a valuable life lesson.

One of my greatest pleasures was when Jack and I set up our arrow-making equipment in his brother-in-law's den. Jack's brother-in-law was a great fellow who always supported our mischief. His den was a mecca for a couple of aspiring outdoorsmen. It was loaded with rifles, pistols, shotguns, reloading equipment, blowguns, boomerangs, bows, crossbows, sling shots, fishing gear, and other outdoor paraphernalia. We would then fletch rabbit arrows up by the dozens while watching all the old great TV cowboy shows: "Have Gun will Travel," "Gunsmoke," "Maverick," etc. Jack's older sister would supply us with sandwiches, potato chips, cake, pop, and ice cream.

During these den sessions, we'd plan our safaris and adventures. We were so involved in hunting and fishing, that we didn't get into too much real trouble. I feel sorry for the boys of today who are often wrapped up in other, less wholesome, precocious things.

One of our better safaris was to drift over the smooth tidal flats on Mission Bay in a ten foot skiff and shoot stingrays and sharks with stout arrows. Another great adventure was hunting ground squirrels in rural San Diego County.

We always carried a wide assortment of bows on our expeditions. Typically, we'd have a couple of yew bows, a lemonwood bow, and various composite bows of both longbow and recurve styles.

Because we looked upon ourselves as adventurers, we would often eat our kills. Rabbits, ground squirrels, doves, and quail were regular fare. An evening campfire in a secluded, subtropical grove was part of the charm of adventuring. Roasted rabbit and potatoes along with fireside conversations was prime entertainment—it still is. During these episodes, we'd feel a kinship with Pope and Young and Ishi and the Thompsons and all mankind that hunted beasts with bow and arrow.

In my teenage years, I yearned to leave the small-game hunting fields and go into the mountains of the far country to hunt big game. Throughout my life, I've been a lover of the great outdoors. I have built campfires all over the west. I can truthfully say that regardless of where I have roamed or wandered, I never had more fun with a bow and arrow than in the times of my youth. Now that I'm much older, I yearn to go back to the days and places of yesteryear. I would have my bow and quiverful of arrows, vigor in my body, a spaniel at my heels, and an adversary in an open, surplus army jeep.

Chapter 21
COCK O' THE WALK

The old "Cock o' the Walk" syndrome—yes, I've seen it manifested in archery many times. I bet you have, too.

I've been an elementary school teacher for well over 20 years and have seen similar manifestations in children. In a classroom of kids, it is common for one or two to become popular for various reasons. These children will form close, exclusive, informal, social groups. When someone outside the group gets any notoriety, the popular "Cocks o' the Walk" in the group say and do mean things to the outsider to keep him or her in place and insure there own social standing.

The first time I observed this in archery was in a city that had a champion archer. This fellow was a great shooter, and he owned a small archery shop. Also, there were two other archery shops in town. One was owned by a very fine, young, Jewish man who was a great shot. The third was owned by a nationally recognized bowmaker. The champion was a big, powerful fellow. He became abusive to the Jewish man. He also called him cruel and prejudicial names in public. Eventually, the Jewish man actually became fearful when he went to the local archery shoots. He finally closed his shop and moved to another town. The third shop owner was verbally maligned by the champ for years, but he never quit business.

Since then, I've observed this behavior many times. One bowyer friend of mine related that a "Cock o' the Walk" shop owner had done similar things to him and his friends. It seems that my friend has a customer who won a longbow shooting title with his bow. The "Cock o' the Walk," in his childish way, proclaimed the shooter, the bowyer, and his bows as unworthy trash. Because of this, my bowyer friend will not attend gatherings where this "Cock o' the Walk" struts.

One summer I went to a longbow shoot. People came from all over the country. The event was put on by a local traditional club. Right away I noticed that the local club members were wearing tee shirts advertising brand "X" longbows. The maker of brand "X" longbows was the club president and "Cock o' the Walk." It soon became evident to a lot of us there, that if you didn't shoot a brand "X," you were an outcast. One outcast shooter ended in a three way tie for a win on one of the events. Because of some chicanery from the brand "X" people, he was given a wrong time for the shoot-off. When he showed up at the appointed time, the shoot-off had already been completed, and he was listed as a defaulted loser. You guessed it! A brand "X" guy won.

I suppose it is hard for a person to walk with his magnificent plumage glistening in the sunlight and not be affected. When you get to be good at something, you may start believing your own press. Pretty soon, everyone is below you. Pride! Many have fallen into its ugly grasp.

In the great plan of life, a person's shooting ability, his hunting trophies, his bows, his bowmaking ability, his memberships in organizations, his ownership of an archery business, or his authorship of archery publications really doesn't amount to that much. What really counts is a person's relationship with his God, family, friends, and community. "For what shall it profit a man if he shall gain the whole world, and lose his own soul?" (St. Mark 8:36)

Traditional archers prefer distinctive hats.

Chapter 22
THE SYLVAN TOXOPHILITE
and the Raiment of the Noggin

There is something that traditional bowmen do that is unique. At large gatherings, such as shoots, it becomes quite obvious! Go into any hunting camp, and it is even more so. I started doing it right after I took up the sport without even realizing the significance of my action. I venture to say that you do it too, if you dabble in the sport any at all.

A while back, I was looking at some pictures of hunting bowmen from the 1940's. It dawned on me that each one expressed his individuality with his hunting hat. Apparently, no two archers wore the same style of hat. This observation interested me. With deliberation, I started my own private research on this hat phenomena. I have drawn some conclusions from my observations. One is that compounders are not too hat conscious. They use a small variety of camouflage hats for the most part. In fact, the more a compounder can dress in the current technological outfits like everyone wears, the better he seems to like it.

Archers, on the other hand, appear to go to great lengths to embellish their craniums. They do not want to be like anyone else. My friend Cecil, for example, wears a silly looking little cowboy hat that is so flat on top, it looks like a plate. It is embarrassing just to be around him. And he wears this hat at every hunt or shoot or greasy spoon joint we attend. Another friend, Louie, wears a weird green felt hat. I believe I knew him two years before he took it off. You see, he lost it at a Michigan longbow shoot. People could not recognize him anymore. Everyone just thought he was a new bare-headed archer that didn't have the courtesy to wear a distinctive hat. A year later, some fellow returned Louie's hat. He found it on the ground surrounded by several vicious dogs that were intent on killing the thing. It was rescued, and this fellow recognized the hat but couldn't remember the face of its owner. At the next Michigan longbow shoot, I was there when it was returned. The fellow was asking every bare-headed archer if they claimed ownership. Louie exclaimed, "It's my hat!" It was a very touching scene. Big tears welled up in Louie's eyes as he took the hat and ceremoniously placed it on his head.

The rest of us immediately said, "Louie, it's you! We wondered where you were."

A similar reckoning happened to Fred Bear. He had a guy who worked for him named Tipton Jones. Tipton looked quite a bit like Fred. So much so, that he was often mistaken for Bear. The saving grace was that Fred always wore a distinctive gentleman's hat. So, it was easier to tell them apart by the hat. Look at the old pictures of Fred Bear, and he will always be recognizable by his hat.

My own hat is a World War I, felt, Australian "Mountie" style. I bought it in a war surplus store in 1965. Like most store-bought stuff, it had to be modified. I narrowed the brim for bowstring clearance and added a leather hatband with an Indian stone arrowhead. I always stick feathers into the band whenever I happen across them in the woods. This fetish application of fresh wild bird feathers brings luck. Whenever I wear my hat at a shoot, people snicker and smile, but I know they are just jealous because they don't have one.

If you are new to the sport, you should consider seriously about this hat business. A good distinctive hat is definitely more important to a traditional shooter than a bow!

The hunting archer has to come to a reckoning when considering how much technology he'll use in his clothing. To me, I feel that the modern "Rambo" camo clothing and my longbow and wooden arrows are incongruous. I prefer to use more conventional clothing—even home made. I know that a number of archers disagree with me, but I have made a choice to wear the time-honored, traditional clothing. Not only is it esthetically pleasing, it is comfortable and often more invisible than the camo stuff that pervades the market.

Chapter 23

MATRIMONY TALES

When I came home the other evening, my wife eyed me suspiciously and said, "Did you get one?"

"No, but let me tell you what happened."

Upon hearing the word "no," tension left and a happy countenance spread across her face. I'm sure there are wives who wish their husbands good luck when they go out hunting. Mine usually says something like, "Don't you shoot a deer today, because we're going out this evening." I guess I can't blame her. I've put her through some extremely trying times. Thinking about some of the archery-related inconveniences I've inflicted upon her, it is a wonder she didn't leave me years ago. But Barbara is a wonderful mate and usually goes along with my madness.

Right after we were married, I was making some arrows. She seemed interested in the fletching I was doing and amused that arrows could be made at home. We lived in a small apartment. After I had a dozen arrows fletched, I went into the kitchen and plugged in my feather burner. Barbara was in the living room watching TV. I adjusted the feather burner and thought that I'd burn one arrow to see how it went and then invite her in to see how it worked. Now, any archer worth his salt knows that one of the real joys in life is when you transform an unruly, feathery shaft into a real arrow with a feather burner. I was anxious to show my bride this magic transformation. I burned the first arrow and was ready to call her when I heard the words, "Oh my gosh! What's that awful smell?" She couldn't be referring to my feather burner could she? This was a great smell. Charging into the kitchen, she took one look and sent me outside faster than she would a peeing puppy. To this day she casts a suspicious eye on me when she sees me with my fletching jigs out.

I let my colors show to Barbara soon after we were married. I fancied myself a good shot on the field range, and so I took her to the Balboa Park field course to exhibit my skills. As we proceeded through the course, my shooting got bad. On the 45-yard target, I blew a shot and became really enraged. I pitched a real third-grade fit. I stomped my foot. It slipped out from under me, and I fell ass over tea kettle on my backside spilling bow and arrows all around. Embarrassed, I tried to quickly get to my feet and slipped once more. To add insult to injury, Barbara howled with laughter. After a minute of cooling off, I could see the humor in my antics also.

This humiliating experience was good for me in the long run. Barbara learned that she was married to someone who has a propensity to make a jackass out of himself, and I learned not to take my shooting too seriously.

As I have said, my wife has always been good to me. Back in 1966 I was going to school and we were as poor as church mice. "Sacrificing" is a good way to describe Barbara. She was, and is, always sacrificing to help her children and me. She wanted to buy me a nice Christmas present and she heard me saying how much I wanted a "Buck" knife. So she squirreled away some money and went down to the local sporting goods store and asked the salesman for a "Buck" knife. He told her that they didn't have a "Buck" knife and then showed her another make and said that it not only worked on bucks but was good for does too. She, knowing that I usually only got does, thought this was a swell knife.

That Christmas when I opened my present and saw the knife I was very pleased, but I wondered why, after so many hints about a "Buck," she had chosen this brand? Very excitedly, she told me that this knife was better than a "Buck" because it could also be used on does. "What?" I asked. She explained it again, this time going into the bit with the salesman. I broke out laughing and had her tell me the story again. Barbara just couldn't comprehend what the joke was. I explained it to her, and she got furious. She would have strangled that salesman right then. I told her not to mind because the knife was a good one. But she

238

insisted on returning it—which I did—and then went to another place and bought a "Buck" knife. I still have that knife. It is one of my prize possessions. I've cleaned many a doe with it (and some bucks, too).

One afternoon a couple of seasons ago, I told Barbara that I was going up behind Camp Govey to one of my favorite spots in the Olympic mountains for an evening hunt. She knew that this place had been good to me in the past, so she quickly said, "Have a good time, but don't get anything. I've been working all day and I'm tired and want to rest this evening."

It was a warm fall evening and I was happy just to get out-doors. Being early in the season, I told myself that I wouldn't shoot anything unless it was a nice buck. Reader, I wish I could take you to this area. What clean air, what wild spectacular scenery, and it was only 40 minutes from my home! The hunt took me down a steep canyon. I was enjoying the splendor of the area and decided to try my predator call. During that time of year, it was very effective on the blacktail deer. After a few calls, I could hear a deer moving in the thick, bushy area below me. For 20 minutes, I called and had that deer moving slowly to-ward me. I couldn't see it, but I knew it was there by its blow-ing. I was really getting excited. It is always thrilling to me to call a wild animal up close. Finally, I started imitating a deer clearing its nostrils by making a couple of blowing sounds. That really did it. Out of the trees, twenty yards away, high stepped a large doe with her hackles up. She was coming straight for me to find out what creature was killing a fawn. I raised my bow when she was ten yards away. She saw me, but it was too late. I released the arrow, and it went down and through her chest cavity.

My first thought was, "What have I done!" Down went the deer as if pole-axed. I looked around. It was practically straight up for one-half a mile to the car, and darkness was settling over the hills. I couldn't haul her out alone. I'd have to go home and get help. "Don't get anything." The words of my wife echoed in my mind. I went home and got the neighbor and his kid and my boy, Matt, to help me drag the deer back to the car. The warm evening called for quick butchering. Like the good sport she is, Barbara stayed up with me while we processed the deer. It was four in the morning when we were finally done.

A gathering of "Kindred Spirits."

Chapter 24
KINDRED SPIRITS

My religious upbringing has taught me that there is opposition in all things: night/day; rich/poor; sickness/health; good/evil, etc. Diversion away from the necessary is bad. If this is true, then I have been diverted from the necessary most of my life. This diversion is archery—not just a "from time-to-time" diversion but a full-time occupation. I have met others with the same shortcoming. I call them "Kindred Spirits." I have met them in all walks of life, from the most humble to the exalted. What is a "Kindred Spirit?" Please, let me define.

Numerous people are bitten by the archery bug. Most recover. Some have recurring attacks, and a few of us are afflicted continually. Typically, someone who is terminally afflicted will begin by reading and devouring all information about the sport. He then finds himself in a lifelong battle learning how to properly shoot a bow and arrow. Saxton Pope, in his book *Hunting with the Bow-and-Arrow,* tells of an old archer trying to perfect his release. He went to his grave still working on it. All of you "Kindred Spirits" know the feeling. I have a friend, George, here in Washington state. He is in his late 60's and has been shooting the longbow most of his life. George is a real good shooter, but he's still trying to overcome some archery errors. Recently, at a shoot, he missed a target he shouldn't have. "Fred, why did I do that? I know better!" he exclaimed. Yes, no matter how long we've been at it, we're always a little off on our forms, and we will work at it until death embraces us. "Kindred Spirits" always die in love with archery and a little off on form.

Back in the mid-1980's Hugh Rich called me and asked if I would make a special longbow for a friend of his. He related that the great trick-shot of the 1940's, Ande Vail, was not doing too well physically. Another friend of Hugh's, Mike Jordon, decided that they ought to buy Ande a nice bow to cheer him up. Now Ande, being a "Kindred Spirit," was really touched by the gift. But illness had its cruel hold on the aging Ande, and he had to be hospitalized. Hugh told me that during those last parts of Ande's life in Boise, Idaho, he would call for his bow and arrows to be brought to his bed where he could look upon them in pleasant reverie. Ande told Hugh that his new bow was the best he ever had and was the nicest of gifts. It seems that "Kindred Spirits" often affect each other in the most considerate ways, and I was very pleased to be part of it.

Another feature of "Kindred Spirits" is that they usually show up at archery events or hang around archery shops. A number of years ago I was spending a warm summer evening on a target range in Seattle. Just before dark, I went to my car to put the equipment away. An old gentleman approached and congratulated me on my shooting. He had been watching me shoot. He told me that he loved shooting, but the frailties of age had forced him to quit. We talked for awhile and then went to local grill where we ate some pie and chatted. I recognized a "Kindred Spirit" right away. He told me that he made most of his tackle, and he had several yew longbows. I was anxious to see them, and he invited me to come to his house later in the week to see his bows.

A grand evening it turned out to be. The old sage took me into his den and told the history of each of his many bows. He picked up an especially beautiful bow. It was one of his favorite hunters. The tight grained yew was polished brightly by many hand-rubbed anointings of oil. The nocks were the traditional horn, masterfully shaped in the classical fashion. The old archer was relating some facts about it, when a far away look came into his aged eyes. He stopped talking for a spell. Once again he was living those days of long ago amongst forest and field. Quietly I waited, then he went on. He showed me his old hunting arrows and other equipment. I was enjoying his companionship immensely; two "Kindred Spirits," one young, one old, feeding on each other's favorite subject.

In 1990, I got personally acquainted with Bob Wesley. I had met him a few years earlier, but it was later, while I was finishing my Master's Degree at the University of Southern Mississippi, that I was able to go to his home in Poplarville, Mississippi, and converse and shoot with him. Bob and I found that we had a lot of similarities, not only being about the same age, we had other commonalities. One evening, as we were talking, it struck us that we were "Kindred Spirits"—two old fools hopelessly in love with the most ancient of sports. I tell you, it is nice to find a bird of a feather that is hooked on archery like oneself. Bob, a real gentleman, can shoot that longbow like nobody else.

When you get to the point where you are eternally enticed into the sport as a "Kindred Spirit," you will start coming across others. They will often appear at the most unexpected times and places.

Maurice Thompson, in *Witchery of Archery,* relates an interesting episode. He and his brother, Will, were practicing on a lawn target when a man of reduced circumstances approached them. He asked for a morsel of food, and the two sent someone to the kitchen. Will and Maurice continued their practice, and the tramp stood watching. Finally he said, "Archery is a noble sport." He then went on to explain that he was a gentleman and had practiced archery before he had fallen on bad times. Then with sincerity in his voice and manner, the tramp asked if he could take a shot. Will handed him his bow and arrow. The vagabond eagerly grasped it and quickly nocked the arrow, shooting it into the very center of the bullseye eye at 40 yards. The Thompson brothers were so taken by this that Will went immediately to the house and came back with a feast. Yes, "Kindred Spirits" sometimes come unexpectedly.

There are a few traditional archery clubs around the country where congregations of "Kindred Spirits" may be found. What a joy it is shooting with them. Oregon has a history of great old clubs. One of the best was the Sylvan Archers. I have found that for the average new comer, their sojourn in the sport is only for two to four years. Therefore, the clubs that have been around awhile and have older members usually have more "Kindred Spirits."

Each avid archer generally will have his own private circles of "Kindred Spirits." They serve a purpose. For me they are often a touchstone to sanity. The rigors of life can be very demanding—as you very well know. The pressures of job, family, church, health, or other things completely bog a person down. When life really gets tough, I often get ahold of a "Kindred Spirit" and spend some time discussing archery or shooting arrows. It is amazing how rejuvenating this can be.

One "Kindred Spirit" I'm acquainted with is a fellow about my age. Like myself, he is always trying to improve equipment. He really is into broadheads and manufactures a great head. Ron Hoiland is his name. We have been hanging around together for many years. Occasionally, we will get together and palaver over our latest projects. We especially like to grab some equipment and go afield, stump-shooting. Our outings take us into many greasy spoon restaurants were we hash over our archery philosophies and ruminate over our meals and let everything else in the world simmer on the back burner.

Chapter 25
CONNECTIONS

An old lady saved my life once. I mean a real old lady. When I was in high school, in 1954, I found out that a bookstore in downtown San Diego had a copy of Saxton Pope's *Hunting with the Bow-and-Arrow*. Right after school one day I went and purchased a copy. I was so excited when I left the store, my mind was elsewhere. I tried to cross the busy city street without paying attention to a car making a right turn in front of me. I felt a hand tug on my shirt and pull me back and saw the blur of a car as it passed. I turned around to the admonishment of a grandma letting me know how I needed to look before I walked, etc.

The book has had a profound impact on me. Now, in later years, I wish I would have paid as much attention to the study of scripture. For some reason, known only to the powers that be, I find a real affinity for this special writing. I still remember my first reading. I was enthralled with the story of Ishi, the romance of deer and bear and mountain lion hunting, and the adventure of bagging grizzly bear. Through this marvelous book I have made some connection with Saxton, Art, the Chief, and Ishi.

Archery has come to us from the foundations of mankind. When we pursue the sport, we share a heritage with untold multitudes of archers through many millennia. Traditional archery helps us feel more connected to all of this. Sometimes it's nice to just sit and ponder these things.

When I was a kid, many of the old archers were still connected to the self-wood bows and wooden-arrow era. What knowledge and stories they possessed! How fortunate I am for tasting a flavor of it. Archery was a completely different game then. In order for a person to become an effective hunting bowman, he had to become very involved with the archer's craft. This often entailed the making of personal equipment. With my fondness for making bows and other equipment, I was delighted to sit and listen to their advice and stories.

One old-timer told me a tale about how he got a deer in San Diego's Mission Valley with his lemonwood bow. I was amazed because the area was covered with homes, but he assured me it was quite wild then. This story has amused me over the years, but it is even more poignant today. A couple of years ago, I shot a deer a few miles down the road. Today, right where I killed the deer, a development has gone in and turned the whole area into housing sites. I imagine that someday I will be telling a youngster that I killed a deer right where all of those houses are.

I remember another old sage quite vividly. He was an old-time bowyer. He had lots of stories, but what I remember most is that this fellow never used any kind of finger protection when he was shooting. He shot heavy longbows, too—in the 70- to 80-pound range! He also had a great love for anybody who was an archer. He had shot most of his life when archers were often a rare commodity, and he felt a kinship with them. As time passed, he became confused by the newer breed of archer that was indoctrinated by commercial propaganda. He evaluated people by their conduct and not by what kind of equipment they used.

During the self-wood bow era, archers got together and reveled in their sport. They loved to wander the hills and fields to shoot. They chased game in fair pursuit for the joy of the hunt. They met at tournament gatherings and enjoyed each others' successes. They were a fraternity of people who had fun playing bows and arrows; often misunderstood by others as being somewhat eccentric or childish. As times changed and commercialism invaded the sport, a lot of old-timers couldn't relate to the newer shooters who were programmed into commercial archery.

The remnants of the self-wood bow era archers are quite rare today. They are all old and they are all gentlemen; at least those that I know are. I met one in Michigan a couple of years ago. He still makes his own wooden longbows and arrows, and he still vigorously hunts deer. The connection I have with his generation adds immense personal enjoyment to the sport. When a gentleman like this looks at a bow, he looks at its beauty. Often, newer archers look at a bow and query on how fast it is. I have one of his handmade hunting arrows. I look at it on the wall and I remember him.

My den walls are adorned with scores of arrows given to me by archers from around the world. They connect me personally with their previous owners. I have a couple of arrows given to me by Rube Powell, five times national field champion during the 1950's, and perhaps the very finest shooter of that, or any, time. My friend, the late Hugh Rich, the great archer and manufacturer, gave me one of his personal hunting arrows. Many of my customers have given me their arrows, and I have a number from the myriad of people I shoot with. I would recommend this arrow collecting to anyone. What great connections!

Sometimes you can get to know someone by going through their stuff. For instance, many years ago, a teacher in my school district had a sudden severe heart attack. I was called in to take his class of 42 fourth-graders for the rest of the year. One of my jobs was to pack up all of his personal effects. As I went through his collection of things accumulated from a lifetime of teaching, I couldn't help but gain a personal insight into this fellow.

My eldest son, Dwain, made friends with an old man in Oregon. This man had once been an avid archer, but sickness and age had forced him to give up the sport. His family did not fully appreciate the old archery equipment that he cherished so much. Knowing that my son had a liking for archery, he gave his stuff to him shortly before he died. Dwain brought it home to me, knowing that it would make a good addition to our den.

The state of Oregon has been a stronghold in traditional archery since at least the 1920's. And so it is today in the 1990's. Oregon has spawned many great archers. One group called themselves "Sylvan Archers." They were a very active group and loved to dress up in Robin Hood attire and play Sherwood Forest.

When I sat down to look at the collection that Dwain had brought, I could see a lot of Oregon archery influence in it. There was the yew hunting bow, so typical of the place and period; several dozen arrows, from target types to broadheads; and quivers, arm guards, and shooting gloves. Old hunting licenses and other assorted things were included. All of these things revealed a picture of the old man. I could see how he sharpened his broadheads, his favorite arrow crest, his draw length, and a multitude of other little things.

I haven't yet decided whether or not I enjoy going through someone's stuff after he has died. There is an intrigue in seeing a person's special treasures, but with me there is a sadness to it also. I feel empathy, and maybe the sadness is for myself, because I will be passing beyond the veil someday, too—then again, maybe it is from something else. Anyway, I feel the connection.

Photographs make great connections. I wish I would have been more oriented towards picture taking in the past. Some friends of mine have wonderful photo collections of archers they have met from around the world.

One summer day I climbed a hill in a wild area of the Northwest. I had been recovering from a serious illness, and being in the outdoors made me feel better. I stopped and looked down at a dusty area on the ground. A glint of sparkle caught my eye and I bent over to examine it. It was an obsidian flake. I looked more closely over the spot and detected it was covered with flakes. Upon further investigation I discovered this area to be a fire pit made by earlier inhabitants. This was a place for them to sit by the fire and overlook the valley as they chipped tools and weapons. I sat myself down under a ponderosa and surveyed the old camp. I could visualize hunters, old and young, sitting before the glowing warmth of a fire. Chunks of elk venison were sizzling. Older warriors were teaching novices how to chip tools. Stories illuminated the night air. I was really connecting with my archery friends from the dust when I slowly came out of my reverie. Somehow this spot left me with a sacred feeling.

I went into an electrical supply store one day to buy some special component. I noticed a small area in one corner of the store that had some primitive masks and weapons displayed. Upon further investigation, I discovered a bow and several arrows made by a primitive tribe from New Guinea. The store owner told me that his missionary friend, who served some time over there, was in terrible financial straights, and he wanted to sell the artifacts. The next thing I knew, I was walking out of the electrical store with the bow and arrows, and two masks in hand. At home I sat and studied the long wooden bow. To most folks it would appear to be simple. As an experienced bowyer I could understand what the bowmaker was thinking when he made it. The workmanship actually exceeds what I see on many bows on today's market. I wonder what its maker would think if he knew that his wonderful bow ended up halfway around the world in another bowmaker's hands. Upon examining the equipment, a feeling of kinship comes over me, and I feel a oneness with this faraway bowmaker.

About twenty years ago, I was sneaking along a hilltop looking for mule deer. The migratory range was full of deer, and I was having the time of my life. The weather was clear and cold, and a skiff of snow dusted the ground. Ponderosa pines dotted the rugged hills, and the nomadic mule deer were coming out of their high mountain homes to spend the winter in the lower hills. As I stalked along I heard a noise to my right. Four deer where bounding away from me in single file twenty yards in front. I raised my bow and pulled on the last one, a nice fat buck. I released the shaft and it went straight for the old boy's ribs. Then thunk! To my surprise, it was sticking into a small, hard stump that I hadn't noticed. The deer disappeared, and I went over to retrieve my arrow. I was astonished to find another arrow in the same little stump! Both arrows were embedded at the very same angle! I extracted them both. The other arrow was a fiberglass shaft tipped with a Bear Razorhead. I still have it today as part of my den's memorabilia. What I really wondered about was the possibility of another hunter getting the same shot with identical results. Was his shot at a nice buck? Did he have the same frustrated feeling? Was he as lucky as me and get another nice deer later in the season?

My fourth-graders came into class the other day all excited— there was to be a snake-man putting on a reptile assembly. My mind drifted on back to another snake-man assembly a number of years earlier—oh, was that something! But, I'm getting ahead of myself. Let me start at the very beginning.

During my teenage years, I had a boa constrictor skin. One day I was at San Diego's "Museum of Man" enjoying the fabulous Jessop collection of primitive archery items. I was impressed with the artful geometric designs that a number of aboriginal people put on their bows. It struck me that the design on my snakeskin was similar to some of the designs on these bows. So I took one of my 69-inch Eicholtz recurve bows, and cut and glued my boa constructor skin to its back. It really turned out quite nice. So good, in fact, that one of my hunting buddies, Ken, had me put a diamondback skin on his 66-inch Eicholtz bow.

We took our bows to a favorite rabbit patch hunting one evening. Ken spied a cottontail in a sandy arroyo. He shot way short, but the arrow skipped across the top of the sand and hit the bunny. It ran into some thick brush, so we laid our bows under some bushes and took off into the chaparral. After we secured the rabbit, we went back for our bows. We couldn't find them. After a five minute search, we discovered them under the bush where we'd laid them. Their snakeskin backings were so well camouflaged that we couldn't see them. Since then, I have consistently used snakeskin backings on my personal hunting bows.

In the early 1980's I was putting snakeskins on some of my commercial bows, but my skin supply was not too good. Then came the snake-man. He arrived at school one afternoon in a big van loaded with exotic reptiles. Evidently, he was a renowned herpetologist that spent a lot of time traveling around the country showing his reptiles to schools.

Well, as he proceeded through his demonstration, I was impressed. All I could see were numerous species of snakes that would make very pleasing bow-backings. When the snake-man was finished, I immediately went up to him. Then I did something very foolish. With all of this guy's expertise I figured he could connect me to where I could get some really exotic skins. So I said to him, "I really enjoyed your show. I make archery bows using snakeskin backings. Would you happen to know of a supplier of snakeskins?" From the look on his face, I could tell that I just asked him a dumb-assed question. He sharply told me about the evils of using snakeskins commercially. I should have known better. Later, I told my wife of my indiscretion. We had a big laugh.

A year later I came home from school one day and my wife told me that I made national television that day. It seems that the snake-man was on one of the network talk shows. He was asked about some of the abuses to snakes, and he told several sordid tales—including one about a bowmaker in Washington state that actually uses snakeskin to decorate archery bows.

Now, my trail of environmental exploitation has been exposed by this national connection.

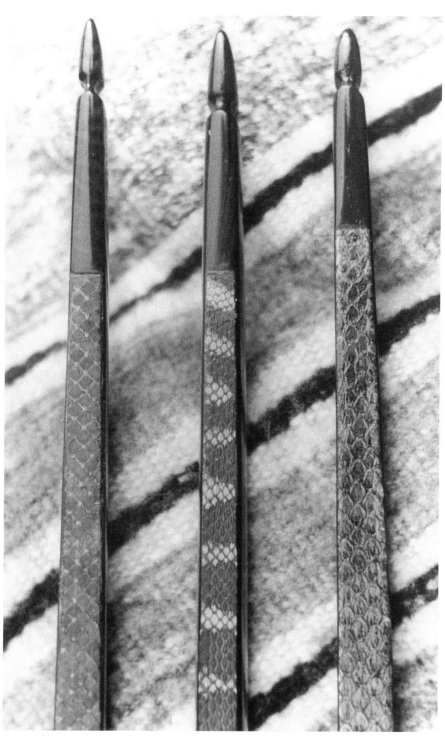

Some of the author's snakeskin bows.

ELDERLY BOWMAN

The house is quiet, and the elderly bowman sits solitarily in his den and gazes at the dozens of photos and mementos decorating the walls. He reflects that so many pictured have passed away. Tomorrow he will go deer hunting up on his favorite evergreen mountain, and he has a dull ache over his soul. Awhile back, his loving mate had also joined the eternities, and his children and grandchildren now live in faraway cities, leaving the elderly bowman empty of spirit and alone in his reverie.

On the morrow, he rises and drives to the evergreen mountain. He parks, and with bow in hand and quiver on his side trudges up his favorite trail, as he had done a multitude of times. He stops and smells the fragrant, clean air and eyes the spectacular scenery. This particular domain has been his exclusively for decades, but this time it seems that the world weighs heavily on his shoulders. There seems little joy now that his old friends are gone, and his wife doesn't grace his home awaiting his return. Going higher into the mountains, the elderly bowman feels a tug of breath. Sitting down, he rests from the climb. His bow is in hand and his arrows are alongside. A golden eagle glides across the sky in front, and a chickaree squirrel barks somewhere below. Clear across a canyon, he spies a black bear breaking open a log searching for a lunch of grubs. The elderly bowman smiles. Yes, the outdoors has always lifted his spirits.

Oh, elderly bowman, close your eyes. Close your eyes and enjoy the moment. Forever is just a nod away!

Open thine eyes now and behold; here comes thy sweet wife to greet thee. Has she ever looked prettier? Take her hand, bowman. Yes, that's right. Now, walk with her through the forest that thou lovest. Don't look down on that remnant of thyself lying upon the grass with bow in hand.

Take thy beautiful companion and proceed with love into the eternities.

EPILOGUE

The sport of traditional archery can be enjoyable from the time one commences with it—no matter how old he is. And as he continues with the sport, great satisfaction may be gleaned. This book represents some of what I've gleaned from nearly one-half century of participation. After reading it, you should see a reflection of the author. Did you find any hidden messages? I have freely placed them throughout and will not be so bold as to reveal them to you—you'll have to ferret out these oracular gems on you own!

There are some reoccurring concepts that are pretty obvious. Begging forgiveness for being repetitious, let me give a final reinforcement. Archery should be fun. Never take yourself so seriously that you forget this. You'll find that your greatest pleasures from the sport come by the discipline you learn using your own basic skills and instincts and not relying on too much technology. From the friends and acquaintances acquired while pursuing the sport, your life will also be enriched. Remember, there are many more important things in life than the ancient game of bows-and-arrows, and you should never let archery interfere with the important things.

On a snowy, winter's day, I followed the tracks of a bowman left in the snow. As they led up a long, hilly ridge, I discovered a drama. I could easily follow his impressions in the snow to where they overlapped those of several deer. He followed the deer's tracks for a ways. I could discern where his feet took a shooting stance and then moved off in a direction of some bushes. Like him, I could see the hair and blood specks. The tracks led to where the deer died and the bowman dressed it. I'm sure this was a happy bowman.

I hope the "Great Spirit" will guide your tracks to many fine adventures, too. May he grant that you will always be able to take the bow and quiver from their peg and go out and dance with your shadow.

ORDER FORM

Order Additional Copies for Your Family and Friends

Yes, please send me _____ copies of

The Traditional Way
The Mystique and Heritage of Archery
by Fred Anderson

@ $22.95 (Includes postage and handling) _____

TOTAL (payment enclosed) _____

Make checks payable to TOX PRESS.

Mail your order today to: TOX PRESS

E 750 Krabbenhoft Rd.
Grapeview, WA 98546

Name _____
Address_____
City _____ State _____ Zip _____

Thank you for your order.

YOUR NOTES

YOUR NOTES

YOUR NOTES